THE JURY AND THE MACHINE:

Artificial Intelligence and the Limits of Algorithmic Adjudication

By Daniel S. Alcorn

Sterling Letter

TABLE OF CONTENTS

INTRODUCTION

As artificial intelligence increasingly predicts judicial decisions, some scholars have begun to ask whether machines could replace juries. This work addresses a question made plausible by machine learning: can artificial intelligence substitute for the jury as a fact-finder in the United States legal system?[1] It is the first to analyze algorithmic jury substitution through the lens of legal epistemology and institutional design rather than constitutional doctrine or algorithmic bias.

The work does not treat that question as constitutional.[2] It does not ask whether jury substitution is permissible under the Sixth or Seventh Amendments,[3] but a more fundamental question: whether substitution is *possible* as a matter of epistemology and technology.[4] If one imagines a legal system free to redesign its institutions, could AI do what jurors do when they decide whether testimony is credible, whether a story is coherent, and whether uncertainty is tolerable under the governing burden of proof?[5]

The work makes three contributions. First, it reconceptualizes the jury not as a constitutional safeguard but as an epistemic institution structured to produce legitimate judgments under uncertainty. Second, it demonstrates that the reasoning central to jury decision-making—credibility assessment, narrative synthesis, and normative evaluation—cannot presently be replicated by systems optimized for statistical prediction. Third, it shows that replacing juries with

---

[1] *See* Ryan Calo, *Artificial Intelligence Policy: A Primer and Roadmap*, 51 U.C. DAVIS L. REV. 399, 401–05 (2017).
[2] *See* id.
[3] *See Duncan v. Louisiana,* 391 U.S. 145, 149-58 (1968).
[4] Larry Laudan, *Truth, Error, and Criminal Law: An Essay in Legal Epistemology* 13–20 (Cambridge University Press 2006).
[5] *See* Harry Surden, *Artificial Intelligence and Law: An Overview*, 35 GA. ST. U. L. REV. 1305, 1310–16 (2019); *See* Valerie P. Hans & Neil Vidmar, *Judging the Jury* 2–9 (1986).

algorithmic decision-makers would transform the institutional logic of the trial from democratic judgment to technocratic optimization.

The jury is often treated as a constitutional relic preserved by the Sixth and Seventh Amendments,[6] a quaint and intentionally inefficient mechanism for civic participation rather than accuracy.[7] Yet this trivializes its deeper role.[8] The jury is the epistemic engine of adjudication: the institution through which courts claim authority to declare what happened and impose binding consequences.[9] It is the legal system's answer to the problem of historical truth under uncertainty, incomplete information, and contested narrative.[10]

Prior scholarship examines algorithmic decision-making in administrative governance and predictive judging, but little considers whether AI could replace the jury as an epistemic institution, and what exists approaches the problem through constitutional or regulatory lenses. This work analyzes it through legal epistemology, drawing on Ronald Allen, Larry Laudan, and Mirjan Damaška to explain how verdicts are produced under irreducible uncertainty, and contributes to jury theory by emphasizing the jury's role as a democratic epistemic institution.

The jury's epistemic function matters because adjudication is retrospective, not predictive.[11] The trial reconstructs past events from partial traces—testimony, documents, forensic artifacts, and memory[12]—and is neither an experiment nor repeatable.[13] The jury must decide, amid irreducible

---

[6] U.S. CONST. amend. VI; U.S. CONST. amend. VII.
[7] *See*, e.g., William G. Young, *Vanishing Trials, Vanishing Juries, Vanishing Constitution*, 40 SUFFOLK U. L. REV. 67, 67–72 (2006).
[8] *See* Akhil Reed Amar, *The Bill of Rights as a Constitution*, 100 YALE L.J. 1131, 1183–88 (1991); *See Duncan*, 391 U.S. at 156.
[9] *See* James B. Thayer, *A Preliminary Treatise on Evidence at the Common Law* 506–10 (1898).
[10] *See* Laudan, *supra* note 4, at 13–20.
[11] *See* Mirjan R. Damaška, *Evidence Law Adrift* 3–10 (1997).
[12] *See id*; *see also* Ronald J. Allen & Brian Leiter, *Naturalized Epistemology and the Law of Evidence*, 87 VA. L. REV. 1491, 1503–08 (2001).
[13] *See* Damaška, *supra* note 11, at 7–10.

ambiguity, which account of reality will be treated as legally true.[14] That decision is not merely descriptive but coercive: it authorizes imprisonment, compels transfers, and confers moral condemnation.[15] The jury's legitimacy has therefore never rested solely on accuracy[16] but on the claim that the jury trial is a fair and socially acceptable mechanism for reaching closure when certainty is unavailable.[17]

The question is easily misunderstood as merely one of computational power.[18] Many assume that if AI can outperform humans in chess and pattern recognition, it can outperform jurors.[19] AI already performs tasks resembling adjudication. Danielle Keats Citron shows that automated governmental decision-making has eroded procedural protections by embedding discretionary judgments in opaque code shielded from review, prompting her call for "technological due process."[20] Predictive policing tools estimate risk,[21] sentencing algorithms forecast recidivism,[22] credit models assign trustworthiness,[23] and employment screening determines who reaches labor markets.[24] Pauline T. Kim shows how such data-driven tools can replicate historical bias through proxies while operating opaquely.[25] These systems are not juries,

---

[14] *See* Laudan, *supra* note 4, at 16–19.
[15] *See In re Winship*, 397 U.S. 358, 363–64 (1970); *See id.*
[16] Hans & Vidmar, *supra* note 6, at 2–9.
[17] *See id*; *see also* Damaška, *supra* note 11, at 10–15.
[18] *See* Surden, *supra* note 5, at 1310–13.
[19] Stuart Russell & Peter Norvig, *Artificial Intelligence: A Modern Approach* 1–7 (4th ed. 2021).
[20] Danielle Keats Citron, *Technological Due Process,* 85 WASH. U.L. REV. 1249, 1253–62 (2008); Id.
[21] *See* Andrew Guthrie Ferguson, *The Rise of Big Data Policing: Surveillance, Race, and the Future of Law Enforcement* 3–9 (2017).
[22] Julia Angwin et al., *Machine Bias*, ProPublica (May 23, 2016), https://www.propublica.org/article/machine-bias-risk-assessments-in-criminal-sentencing.
[23] *See* Frank Pasquale, *The Black Box Society: The Secret Algorithms That Control Money and Information* 19–26 (2015).
[24] *See* Pauline T. Kim, *Data-Driven Discrimination at Work*, 58 WM. & MARY L. REV. 857, 860–72 (2017).
[25] Id.

but they already convert complex inputs into consequential outputs under uncertainty,[26] making the "AI jury" appear a logical extension of algorithmic governance.[27]

Yet the jury is not simply a pattern-recognition or evidence-weighting device.[28] It performs a hybrid judgment blending inference, narrative construction, credibility assessment, moral evaluation, and social legitimacy.[29] It decides not what is statistically probable but what is sufficiently proven to justify coercion, believable in light of human experience, blameworthy, and reasonable by community norms.[30] The verdict is thus both an epistemic conclusion and a normative act: the jury does not merely *discover* truth but institutionalizes a version of truth as legally binding,[31] inseparable from the moral authority of the state.[32]

To ask whether AI can substitute, one must understand what juries do.[33] Jury decision-making is not arithmetic.[34] Empirical scholarship shows jurors reason through narratives, heuristics, and deliberation rather than probability calculation[35]—story-driven, value-laden, and context-sensitive.[36] The legal system is structured around that cognition,[37] channeling human

---

26 *See* Citron, *supra* note 20, at 1253–62.
27 *See* Surden, *supra* note 5, at 1310–16; *See* Frank Pasquale, *A Rule of Persons, Not Machines: The Limits of Legal Automation*, 87 GEO. WASH. L. REV. 1, 3–10 (2019).
28 *See* Hans & Vidmar, *supra* note 6, at 2–9.
29 *See* Reid Hastie, Steven D. Penrod & Nancy Pennington, *Inside the Jury* 1–10 (Harvard Univ. Press 1983).
30 *See id*; *see also* Damaška, *supra* note 11, at 7–15.
31 H.L.A. Hart, *The Concept of Law* 124–36 (3d ed. 2012); *See* Damaška, *supra* note 11, at 7–10.
32 *See Winship*, 397 U.S. at 363–64.
33 *See* Hastie et al., *supra* note 29, at 1–10.
34 *See id.*
35 *See id.* at 13–28; Amos Tversky & Daniel Kahneman, Judgment Under Uncertainty: Heuristics and Biases, 185 *Science* 1124, 1124–31 (1974).
36 *See id.*
37 *See* Hans & Vidmar, *supra* note 6, at 2–9.

limitation through adversarial presentation, evidentiary rules, burdens of proof, and deliberation.[38] The jury trial is a technology of disciplined human reasoning.[39]

Modern large language models ("LLMs") superficially resemble this narrative reasoning.[40] They summarize testimony, reconstruct timelines, identify contradictions, and generate plausible causal accounts from thousands of pages,[41] which is precisely the danger.[42] LLMs are prone to hallucination, producing false assertions with confident fluency;[43] they lack grounding in the world[44] and do not "know" facts but predict linguistic patterns.[45] Their outputs are epistemically unstable even when persuasive—and persuasion is the currency of trial.[46] For substitution, this instability is potentially catastrophic.[47] The jury's role is to decide whether a narrative is true enough, under law, to justify punishment.[48] The cost of error is severe,[49] and the jury is the central filter.[50] If AI cannot distinguish truth from plausibility, it cannot replace that filter without turning trials into sophisticated speculation.[51]

---

[38] See Fed. R. Evid. 401–403; Fed. R. Evid. 802.
[39] *See* Damaška, *supra* note 11, at 7–15.
[40] Jason Wei et al., Emergent Abilities of Large Language Models, 2022 *Transactions on Machine Learning Research* 1, 1–6 (2022).
[41] *See id*; *see also* Surden, *supra* note 5, at 1310–16.
[42] *See* Pasquale, *supra* note 23, at 10–18.
[43] *See* Surden, *supra* note 5, at 1315–23; Shirin Nilizadeh et al., Measuring and Mitigating Hallucinations in Large Language Models, 56 *ACM Computing Surveys* (forthcoming 2023).
[44] *See* Emily M. Bender et al., On the Dangers of Stochastic Parrots: Can Language Models Be Too Big?, in *Proceedings of the 2021 ACM Conference on Fairness, Accountability, and Transparency* 610, 610–23 (Assoc. Comput. Mach. 2021).
[45] *See id.*
[46] *See* Hastie et al., *supra* note 29, at 13–28.
[47] *See* Laudan, *supra* note 4, at 16–20.
[48] *See Winship*, 397 U.S. at 363–64.
[49] *See id.*
[50] *See id*; *see also* Fed. R. Crim. P. 29.
[51] *See* Pasquale, *supra* note 23, at 10–18; *See* Laudan, *supra* note 4, at 13–20.

The deeper obstacle is judgment, not hallucination.[52] Legal fact-finding is normative.[53] Reasonableness, proximate cause, intent, and recklessness require applying community values[54] not reducible to statistical inference.[55] AI can approximate moral language, but whether it can *exercise* moral judgment is deeply contested,[56] and even if it could, it would lack the moral accountability that makes jury verdicts legitimate acts of collective responsibility.[57] Jury fact-finding is also social: a lay body representing the community[58] confers legitimacy precisely through civic participation.[59] The verdict is accepted not only because it is accurate but because it is publicly intelligible and socially trusted.[60] AI lacks this legitimacy.[61] Even if more accurate, replacing juries with AI would convert adjudication from a democratic process into a technocratic one, shifting authority from citizens to systems that cannot be morally responsible.[62]

This Article argues that AI cannot currently substitute for the jury because the jury performs a hybrid epistemic function AI cannot replicate.[63] Contemporary AI excels at pattern recognition and probabilistic inference but lacks the normative judgment, contextual interpretation, and democratic legitimacy fact-finding requires.[64] It cannot reliably assess

---

[52] *See* Hart, *supra* note 31, at 124–36.
[53] *See id.*.
[54] *See* Restatement (Second) of Torts § 283 (Am. L. Inst. 1965) (reasonable person standard); Restatement (Second) of Torts § 431 (Am. L. Inst. 1965) (legal cause).
[55] *See* Hart, *supra* note 31, at 124–36; *See id.*
[56] John R. Searle, Minds, Brains, and Programs, 3 *Behav. & Brain Sci.* 417, 417–24 (1980).
[57] *See* Hart, *supra* note 31, at 124–36.
[58] *See* Hans & Vidmar, *supra* note 6, at 2–9; *See Duncan*, 391 U.S. at 156.
[59] *See id.*.
[60] *See* Hans & Vidmar, *supra* note 6, at 2–9.
[61] *See* Pasquale, *supra* note 23, at 10–18.
[62] *See id.*
[63] *See* Laudan, *supra* note 4, at 13–20.
[64] *See* Pasquale, *supra* note 23, at 10–18.

credibility,[65] bear moral responsibility for punishment,[66] or generate procedural legitimacy through participation.[67] The best near-term role for AI is augmentation, not substitution: it can help jurors manage complex evidence, but ultimate judgment must remain human—because human judgment is the legal system's mechanism of accountability.[68] This is not an appeal to tradition but an epistemological claim: legal truth is not merely computed but constructed through institutional procedure and human judgment,[69] and judgment, in its present form, is not programmable.[70]

I. THE JURY AS AN EPISTEMIC INSTITUTION

A. The Jury's Function Is Not "Fact-Finding" in a Scientific Sense

The term "fact-finder" suggests scientific investigation—objective inquiry through measurement, experiment, and repeatable verification.[71] But trial fact-finding differs fundamentally.[72] The trial cannot be repeated under controlled conditions;[73] it is a retrospective reconstruction inferred from incomplete evidence filtered through adversarial selection and evidentiary exclusion.[74] The jury's task is not to *measure* reality but to reconstruct a plausible historical account under legal constraints[75]—epistemically closer to historiography than science.[76]

---

65 *See* Hastie et al., *supra* note 29, at 1–10.
66 *See Winship*, 397 U.S. at 363–64.
67 *See Duncan*, 391 U.S. at 156.
68 *See* Citron, *supra* note 20, at 1253–62.
69 *See* Laudan, *supra* note 4, at 13–20; *See* Damaška, *supra* note 11, at 7–15.
70 *See* Searle, *supra* note 56, at 417–24.
71 *See* Karl R. Popper, *The Logic of Scientific Discovery* 27–33 (1959).
72 *See* Damaška, *supra* note 11, at 7–10.
73 *See id.*
74 *See id.*
75 *See* Laudan, *supra* note 4, at 16–20.
76 *See* R.G. Collingwood, *The Idea of History* 231–49 (rev. ed. 1994).

Its product is not absolute truth but a conclusion the system treats as true for liability and punishment.[77]

Karl Popper argued that science advances through falsification, winnowing false theories by testing them.[78] Trial fact-finding is the opposite: trials rarely falsify a narrative.[79] Each side presents a theory, and the jury selects the one best fitting the admissible evidence.[80] The verdict is a selection, not a falsification—a declaration that one account is more convincing and sufficient under the burden of proof.[81] The trial is thus not a scientific truth-discovery mechanism but a structured process for producing closure when certainty is impossible.[82]

The evidentiary rules reflect this compromise: the law excludes evidence not because it is irrelevant to truth but because it is unreliable, prejudicial, or socially undesirable.[83] A jury sees only what survives the filters of relevance, privilege, hearsay, and prejudice,[84] deciding what happened within an artificial evidentiary world constructed by law[85]—not identical to reality, yet treated as binding truth.[86] Jury decision-making is thus interpretive: the jury does not excavate buried facts[87] but constructs a coherent account from what the law permits, what the parties present, and what cognition can synthesize.[88] It is an epistemic institution not because it is perfectly

---

[77] *See Winship*, 397 U.S. at 363–64.
[78] *See* Popper, *supra* note 71, at 27–33; *See id.*
[79] *See* Hastie et al., *supra* note 29, at 13–28.
[80] *See id.*
[81] *See* Laudan, *supra* note 4, at 16–20.
[82] *See* Hans & Vidmar, *supra* note 6, at 2–9; *See* Ronald J. Allen, *A Reconceptualization of Civil Trials*, 66 B.U. L. REV. 401, 401–12 (1986).
[83] *See id*; Fed. R. Evid. 403.
[84] Fed. R. Evid. 802; Fed. R. Evid. 501.
[85] *See* Damaška, *supra* note 11, at 7–15.
[86] *See id.*
[87] *See* Allen & Leiter, *supra* note 12, at 1503–08.
[88] *See* Hastie et al., *supra* note 29, at 13–28.

accurate but because it produces conclusions the system treats as authoritative[89]—its value lying in institutional legitimacy rather than scientific certainty.[90]

B. The Jury as a Credibility-Assessment Mechanism

Assessing credibility is among the jury's most important functions.[91] Courts instruct jurors that they are the "sole judges of the credibility of witnesses,"[92] because trials are frequently contests between competing testimony where documents are incomplete and physical evidence ambiguous.[93] Testimony becomes the primary source from which jurors infer intent, causation, and responsibility;[94] often the decisive question is whom the jury believes.[95]

Credibility involves far more than lie detection: perception, memory, narration, sincerity, and bias.[96] These are not discrete computable variables but intertwined features of human cognition.[97] A witness may sincerely believe a false memory, speak inconsistently from anxiety, or be confidently mistaken.[98] Credibility assessment therefore requires interpreting behavior in context, not merely detecting deception.[99] Humans are poor lie detectors—meta-analyses put accuracy only slightly above chance[100]—yet juries remain tasked with credibility because the system lacks a more

---

[89] *See* Damaška, *supra* note 11, at 7–15.
[90] *See* Hans & Vidmar, *supra* note 6, at 2–9.
[91] *See United States v. Scheffer*, 523 U.S. 303, 313 (1998).
[92] *See* 1A Kevin F. O'Malley, Jay E. Grenig & William C. Lee, *Federal Jury Practice and Instructions* § 15:01 (6th ed. 2024).
[93] *See Scheffer*, 523 U.S. at 313; *See* Damaška, *supra* note 11, at 7–15.
[94] *See Scheffer*, 523 U.S. at 313.
[95] *See id.*
[96] *See* Hastie et al., *supra* note 29, at 13–28; *See id.*
[97] *See id*; *See* Daniel L. Schacter, *The Seven Sins of Memory: How the Mind Forgets and Remembers* 5–12 (2001).
[98] *See id.*
[99] *See id.*
[100] *See* Aldert Vrij, *Detecting Lies and Deceit: Pitfalls and Opportunities* 1–12 (2d ed. 2008); Bella M. DePaulo et al., Cues to Deception, 129 *Psychol. Bull.* 74, 74–118 (2003).

legitimate mechanism.[101] Expert testimony on credibility is disfavored,[102] and the jury's legitimacy rests on the idea that ordinary citizens can determine whom to believe.[103]

Credibility judgment is also shaped by demeanor, tone, and confidence.[104] Courts permit juries to weigh "the manner and demeanor of the witness,"[105] yet demeanor evidence is controversial:[106] jurors often misread it, confidence correlates weakly with accuracy, and trauma, cultural difference, and neurodivergence distort demeanor.[107] Still the jury persists, because credibility is about trust, which is socially defined.[108] This creates a difficulty for AI: a machine might flag statistical markers of deception but cannot distinguish dishonesty from ordinary cognitive imperfection.[109] A credibility judgment requires interpretation—deciding what inconsistencies mean and whether a presentation fits ordinary experience[110]—which the jury does imperfectly but legitimately.[111] AI has not shown it can replicate that legitimacy.[112]

C. The Jury as a Narrative Synthesizer

Humans reason through stories.[113] Jurors do not store evidence as isolated propositions[114] but integrate testimony and exhibits into narratives.[115] The influential "Story Model" holds that

---

[101] *See Scheffer*, 523 U.S. at 313.
[102] *See id.* at 313–17.
[103] *See Duncan*, 391 U.S. at 156; See Hans & Vidmar, *supra* note 6, at 2–9.
[104] *See* O'Malley et al., *supra* note 92, § 15:01.
[105] *See Anderson v. City of Bessemer City*, 470 U.S. 564, 575 (1985).
[106] *See* Jeremy A. Blumenthal, *A Wipe of the Hands, a Lick of the Lips: The Validity of Demeanor Evidence in Assessing Witness Credibility*, 72 NEB. L. REV. 1157, 1157–1223 (1993).
[107] *See id*; *see also* Elizabeth F. Loftus, *Eyewitness Testimony* 19–35 (rev. ed. 1996).
[108] *See* Hans & Vidmar, *supra* note 6, at 2–9.
[109] *See* DePaulo et al., *supra* note 101, at 74–118.
[110] *See* Hastie et al., *supra* note 29, at 13–28.
[111] See *Scheffer*, 523 U.S. at 313.
[112] *See* Pasquale, *supra* note 23, at 10–18.
[113] *See* Hastie et al., *supra* note 29, at 13–28.
[114] *See id.*
[115] *See id.*

jurors construct a story and compare it to verdict categories, selecting the account that feels most coherent and plausible rather than aggregating probabilities.[116] This narrative cognition is an adaptive feature, not a defect:[117] it transforms the piecemeal, out-of-order chaos of trial evidence into coherence.[118] The adversarial system exploits this, presenting evidence as competing narratives through openings, examinations, and closings.[119]

A verdict is thus the adoption of one story over another as the binding account of reality.[120] Credibility and narrative coherence intertwine: jurors believe the story that fits how people behave,[121] and the system's doctrines assume this reasoning.[122] The jury trial is built for story-driven minds, not Bayesian calculators.[123] This bears directly on substitution, because LLMs are powerful narrative engines[124] that may seem suited to the jury's synthesizing role.[125] But narrative synthesis is not truth.[126] AI's narrative competence may create an illusion of reliability even when its output is a plausible story untethered to reality.[127] The jury's synthesis is constrained by common sense and moral accountability; AI's is constrained by statistical plausibility and training data.[128] What looks like the jury's function may be only an imitation of its outward form.[129]

D. The Jury as a Moral and Social Interpreter

---

[116] *See* Nancy Pennington & Reid Hastie, Evidence Evaluation in Complex Decision Making, 51 *J. Personality & Soc. Psychol.* 242, 242–58 (1986); *See id.*.
[117] *See* Jerome Bruner, *Actual Minds, Possible Worlds* 11–25 (1986).
[118] *See id.*; *See* Hastie et al., *supra* note 29, at 13–28.
[119] *See* Blume et al., *supra* note 108, at 1071–82; See id.
[120] *See* Pennington & Hastie, *supra* note 116, at 242–58.
[121] *See* Hastie et al., *supra* note 29, at 13–28.
[122] *See* Blume et al., *supra* note 108, at 1071–82.
[123] *See* Tversky & Kahneman, *supra* note 36, at 1124–31.
[124] See Wei et al., *supra* note 40, at 1–6.
[125] *See id.*
[126] *See* Laudan, *supra* note 4, at 16–20.
[127] *See* Bender et al., *supra* note 44, at 610–23.
[128] *See id.*
[129] *See* Pasquale, *supra* note 23, at 10–18.

The jury's fact-finding blends into moral judgment.[130] Many legal categories are normative rather than descriptive: negligence asks whether conduct was "reasonable,"[131] defamation whether speech was "reckless,"[132] punitive damages whether misconduct was "willful and wanton,"[133] and criminal cases require inferring intent, malice, or depravity.[134] These are moralized assessments requiring jurors to apply community standards and decide what society will tolerate.[135] The jury is thus a moral interpreter, translating abstract law into a judgment about blame,[136] so the verdict operates as both a finding of truth and a social condemnation or vindication[137]—the "conscience of the community."[138] When a jury convicts, it declares guilt proven to a degree justifying punishment, not merely probable.[139]

In *In re Winship*, the Court held that due process requires proof of every element beyond a reasonable doubt, underscoring that the jury finds facts under a constitutionally mandated certitude protecting liberty and public confidence[140]—a moral declaration.[141] The jury is also democratic: Tocqueville called it "a political institution" educating citizens in self-government.[142] Through service, citizens exercise state power and learn the weight of judgment,[143] a civic function inseparable from the epistemic one.[144] The jury ensures that ordinary citizens, not remote officials,

---

[130] *See Duncan*, 391 U.S. at 156.
[131] *See* Hart, *supra* note 31, at 124–36; Restatement (Second) of Torts § 283 (Am. L. Inst. 1965).
[132] *See N.Y. Times Co. v. Sullivan*, 376 U.S. 254, 279–80 (1964).
[133] *See BMW of N. Am., Inc. v. Gore*, 517 U.S. 559, 568 (1996).
[134] *See Morissette v. United States*, 342 U.S. 246, 250–63 (1952).
[135] See Fletcher, *supra* note 56, at 113–25; *See Duncan*, 391 U.S. at 156.
[136] *See id*; *See* Hart, *supra* note 31, at 124–36.
[137] See *Winship*, 397 U.S. at 363–64.
[138] See *Duncan*, 391 U.S. at 156.
[139] *See id.*; *See Winship*, 397 U.S. at 363–64.
[140] Id; *See id.*
[141] *See id.*.
[142] 1 Alexis de Tocqueville, Democracy in America 262–64 (1835).
[143] *See id*; *See id.*
[144] *See Duncan*, 391 U.S. at 156.

authorize coercion.[145] This legitimacy is what AI lacks.[146] A machine verdict would be experienced as imposed, its authority deriving from technical expertise rather than civic participation,[147] converting the trial from a democratic ritual into technocratic classification.[148] The jury's moral function is part of the logic by which the system justifies coercion[149]—a justification AI substitution threatens to sever.[150]

E. The Jury as a Collective Bias-Filtering Device

The jury mitigates individual bias through collective deliberation.[151] The system does not entrust one citizen with the power to convict but distributes it across a group,[152] reflecting the judgment that collective reasoning filters individual error.[153] Deliberation forces jurors to justify beliefs, confront alternatives, and test intuitions against others.[154] Group decision-making has flaws—groupthink, polarization, conformity, and dominance by confident personalities can amplify bias[155]—yet studies suggest deliberation often improves decisions when jurors disagree initially and must give reasons.[156] The jury is an epistemic compromise: a structured collective process for stable conclusions under uncertainty.[157]

---

[145] *See id.*
[146] *See* Pasquale, *supra* note 23, at 10–18.
[147] *See id.*
[148] *See id.*
[149] *See* Amar, *supra* note 8, at 1183–88.
[150] See Pasquale, *supra* note 23, at 10–18.
[151] *See* Hans & Vidmar, *supra* note 6, at 2–9.
[152] *See Williams v. Florida*, 399 U.S. 78, 100 (1970); *See id.*
[153] *See* Hans & Vidmar, *supra* note 6, at 2–9.
[154] *See* Hastie et al., *supra* note 29, at 13–28; *See id.*.
[155] *See* Irving L. Janis, *Groupthink: Psychological Studies of Policy Decisions and Fiascoes* 9–18 (2d ed. 1982); *See* Cass R. Sunstein, *Deliberative Trouble? Why Groups Go to Extremes*, 110 YALE L.J. 71, 71–120 (2000).
[156] *See* Hastie *et al., supra* note 29, at 13–28.
[157] *See* Hans & Vidmar, *supra* note 6, at 2–9.

This matters for substitution. An AI system may appear more consistent, but consistency is not accuracy or justice.[158] A consistent system can consistently err, while a jury's variability may reflect legitimate moral disagreement the system deliberately tolerates.[159] The bias-filtering function is political as well as statistical: it disperses responsibility and prevents legal truth from becoming the product of centralized authority.[160] It is also linked to accountability. When a jury convicts, the community is responsible; were an AI to convict, responsibility would diffuse among programmer, vendor, judge, state, and dataset.[161] The jury makes decisions traceable to accountable human beings[162]—itself a mechanism of legitimacy.[163]

F. What Juries Do Well

Modern literature treats the jury not as a "black box" of arbitrary decision-making but as a systematically understandable institution.[164] Several themes recur: juries are generally competent fact-finders who track "reasonable" outcomes, including those judges would reach;[165] decision-making is narrative-driven;[166] deliberation shapes verdicts through persuasion and collective reasoning;[167] juries are predictably imperfect, with structured weaknesses in handling technical evidence and converting moral judgments into numbers;[168] and juries inject community norms and

---

[158] *See* Pasquale, *supra* note 23, at 19–26.
[159] *See Duncan*, 391 U.S. at 156.
[160] *See* Amar, *supra* note 8, at 1183–88.
[161] *See* Citron, *supra* note 20, at 1253–62.
[162] *See Duncan*, 391 U.S. at 156.
[163] *See* Hans & Vidmar, *supra* note 6, at 2–9.
[164] See Harry Kalven, Jr. & Hans Zeisel, *The American Jury* (1966); Hans & Vidmar, supra note 6, at 2-9.
[165] *See* Kalven & Zeisel, *supra* note 164, at 55–65; *See id.*
[166] *See* Hastie et al., *supra* note 29, at 13–28.
[167] *See id.*
[168] *See* Neil Vidmar & Valerie P. Hans, *American Juries: The Verdict* 215–48 (Prometheus Books 2007); *see also* Cass R. Sunstein et al., *Punitive Damages: How Juries Decide* 3–17 (Univ. of Chi. Press 2002).

democratic legitimacy into adjudication.[169] In *Duncan v. Louisiana*, the Court held the jury-trial right fundamental and incorporated against the states, emphasizing the jury's historic role against governmental oppression.[170]

This literature converges: juries are human, social, and imperfect, but far more rational and defensible than critics assume.[171] It rests on a developed empirical record—Kalven and Zeisel finding juries generally track judicial expectations, diverging mainly in close credibility cases;[172] Hans and Vidmar rebutting claims of incompetence;[173] Diamond's portrait of competent collective error-correction alongside genuine comprehension limits;[174] the Hastie-Penrod-Pennington "story model";[175] Devine's account of jury behavior as scientifically intelligible;[176] and Sunstein and coauthors showing punitive-damages volatility reflects the difficulty of translating shared moral judgment into dollars.[177]

II. LEGAL FACT-FINDING AND THE EPISTEMOLOGY OF PROOF

A. Legal Proof as a Procedural Epistemology

Legal proof is not metaphysical.[178] It is procedural: truth is what can be established under the rules of litigation.[179] This is an institutional necessity, since courts cannot wait for certainty

---

[169] *See Duncan*, 391 U.S. at 156; see also de Tocqueville, *supra* note 142, at 262–64.
[170] *Duncan*, 391 U.S. at 156; *See id.*.
[171] *See* Kalven & Zeisel, *supra* note 164, at 55–65; Hans & Vidmar, *supra* note 6, at 2–9.
[172] Kalven & Zeisel, *supra* note 164, at 3–15; *Id.* at 55–65, 164–77.
[173] Hans & Vidmar, *supra* note 6, at 1–20; *Id.* at 21–60.
[174] *See id.* at 1–20; Diamond, *supra* note 164, at 717–23.
[175] Hastie, et al., *supra* note 29, at 1–25; *Id.* at 25–60.
[176] Dennis J. Devine, *Jury Decision Making: The State of the Science* 1–12 (2012); *Id.* at 13–60.
[177] Sunstein, et al, *supra* note 168, at 1-20; *Id.* at 21–65.
[178] *See* Ronald J. Allen & Michael S. Pardo, *The Problematic Value of Mathematical Models of Evidence*, 36 J. LEGAL STUD. 107, 109–12 (2007); *See* Laudan, *supra* note 4, at 26-32.
[179] *See id.* at 13–20; *see also* Thayer, supra note 9, at 266–68.

and must decide on finite evidence within bounded time.[180] The trial produces knowledge inseparable from the process that generates it[181]—the verdict declares not what "really happened" but what has been proven within a structured adversarial system designed to approximate truth while preserving legitimacy.[182]

This explains why the system treats imperfect outcomes as true.[183] A guilty defendant may be acquitted because evidence was excluded or the burden unmet;[184] a genuinely harmed plaintiff may fail for want of admissible causation evidence.[185] These are the predictable results of a system balancing truth-seeking against fairness, reliability, and dignity[186]—preferring a procedurally justified conclusion to an accurate one reached illegitimately.[187] Laudan and other legal epistemologists describe the trial as a truth-seeking institution constrained by procedural values, arguing criminal procedure should be judged by how well it minimizes error and reframing adjudication as a problem of error distribution between wrongful conviction and wrongful acquittal.[188]

This framing is critical for substitution.[189] If the goal were merely accuracy, one might replace juries with any better predictor.[190] But the trial's objective is institutional justification, not

---

[180] *See* Laudan, *supra* note 4, at 13–20; *See id.* at 26–32.
[181] *See* Damaška, *supra* note 11, at 1331–38; Laudan, *supra* note 4, at 13–20.
[182] *See* Lon L. Fuller, The Adversary System, in *Talks on American Law* 34, 38–44; *see also Duncan*, 391 U.S. at 156.
[183] *See* Laudan, *supra* note 4, at 35–44.
[184] *See Mapp v. Ohio*, 367 U.S. 643, 655–57 (1961); *see also Winship*, 397 U.S. at 363–64.
[185] *See* Restatement (Second) of Torts § 431 (Am. L. Inst. 1965) (causation requirements); *see also Celotex Corp. v. Catrett*, 477 U.S. 317, 322–23 (1986).
[186] *See* Laudan, *supra* note 4, at 35–44; *See* Fed. R. Evid. 403.
[187] *See Winship*, 397 U.S. at 363–64; *see also Mapp*, 367 U.S. at 655–57.
[188] *See* Laudan, *supra* note 4, at 13–20; *see also* Michael S. Pardo, *The Nature and Purpose of Evidence Theory*, 66 VAND. L. REV. 547, 553–60 (2013).
[189] *See* Pasquale, *supra* note 28, at 10–18.
[190] *See* Russell & Norvig, supra note 19, at 1–10.

prediction.[191] The verdict is accepted because it emerges from a process society deems fair enough to justify coercion.[192] Any replacement must therefore replicate not only inference but the procedural legitimacy that makes inference binding.[193] As Susan Haack argues, legal fact-finding reflects a common-sense epistemology grounded in fallibilism and inference to the best explanation, in which burdens and admissibility rules are normative judgments about risk and error distribution rather than pure truth-tracking mechanisms.[194] Legal proof is thus not reducible to computation, which presupposes stable inputs and metrics;[195] the trial is structured by contestation, strategic presentation, and attacks on credibility.[196] The jury's function is not to process information but to render a judgment transforming contested evidence into an enforceable outcome—institutionalized authority, not merely epistemics.[197]

B. Burdens of Proof as Epistemic Thresholds

Burdens of proof are best understood as epistemic thresholds: formalized statements of how much uncertainty society tolerates before authorizing consequences.[198] Preponderance reflects a low threshold;[199] clear and convincing a higher one in contexts like fraud or termination

---

[191] *See* Laurence H. Tribe, Trial by Mathematics: *Precision and Ritual in the Legal Process*, 84 HARV. L. REV. 1329, 1330–35 (1971); *See* Frederick Schauer, *Giving Reasons*, 47 STAN. L. REV. 633, 633–59 (1995).
[192] *See Duncan*, 391 U.S. at 156*; see also Winship*, 397 U.S. at 363–64.
[193] *See* Pasquale, *supra* note 23, at 10–18; Tribe, *supra* note 191, at 1374–76.
[194] Susan Haack, *Epistemology Legalized*, 49 American Journal of Jurisprudence 43 (2004); Id.
[195] *See* Allen & Pardo, *supra* note 178, at 116–21; *See* Judea Pearl, *Causality: Models, Reasoning, and Inference* 1–18 (2d ed. 2009).
[196] *See* Fuller, *supra* note 182, at 38–44; *See id.*
[197] *See* Nancy Pennington & Reid Hastie, *A Cognitive Theory of Juror Decision Making: The Story Model*, 13 CARDOZO L. REV. 519, 525–34 (1991); *See* Mirjan R. Damaška, *The Faces of Justice and State Authority* 3–10 (Yale Univ. Press 1986).
[198] *See* Laudan, *supra* note 4, at 26-32; Allen & Pardo, *supra* note 178, at 109–16.
[199] *See Herman & MacLean v. Huddleston*, 459 U.S. 375, 390 (1983); see also *Concrete Pipe & Prods. of Cal., Inc. v. Constr. Laborers Pension Tr.*, 508 U.S. 602, 622 (1993).

of parental rights;[200] and beyond a reasonable doubt the highest, reflecting the principle that wrongful conviction is worse than wrongful acquittal.[201] These burdens are not statistical.[202] Courts resist translating them into numeric probabilities,[203] because they are normative decision rules embodying moral judgments about risk allocation:[204] the criminal burden expresses a posture that the state must hesitate before condemning and tolerate uncertainty rather than punish on suspicion.[205]

This moral posture challenges substitution.[206] AI systems are optimization systems producing outputs from statistical likelihoods and learned correlations;[207] they do not hesitate in the moral sense.[208] They can output uncertainty numerically but cannot experience the ethical weight reasonable doubt imposes.[209] That standard is a cognitive instruction to restrain closure when doubt persists—as much a feature of moral psychology as of inference.[210] Burdens also serve an expressive function, signaling the seriousness of the outcome: preponderance accepts symmetrical error risk, reasonable doubt errs toward liberty.[211] These are moral commitments, not

---

200 *See Addington v. Texas*, 441 U.S. 418, 424 (1979); *Santosky v. Kramer*, 455 U.S. 745, 769–70 (1982).
201 *See Winship*, 397 U.S. at 363–64; 4 William Blackstone, *Commentaries on the Laws of England* 358 (1769).
202 *See* Allen & Pardo, *supra* note 178, at 109–16.
203 *See Victor v. Nebraska*, 511 U.S. 1, 5–6 (1994); *see also United States v. Frazier*, 387 F.3d 1244, 1270–71 (11th Cir. 2004).
204 *See id.* at 1374–76; *See Addington*, 441 U.S. at 423–24.
205 *See Winship*, 397 U.S. at 363–64; *See id.*
206 *See* Pasquale, *supra* note 28, at 10–18.
207 *See* Russell & Norvig, *supra* note 19, at 1–10; *See* Kevin P. Murphy, *Machine Learning: A Probabilistic Perspective* 1–12 (2012).
208 *See* Searle, *supra* note 56, at 417–24.
209 *See Winship*, 397 U.S. at 363–64; Pasquale, *supra* note 14, at 10–18.
210 See *Victor*, 511 U.S. at 5–6; Fed. Jud. Ctr., *Pattern Criminal Jury Instructions* 17–18 (1987) ("firmly convinced" language).
211 *See* Dan M. Kahan, *The Supreme Court 2010 Term—Foreword: Neutral Principles, Motivated Cognition, and Some Problems for Constitutional Law*, 125 HARV. L. REV. 1, 19–26 (2011); Tribe, *supra* note 6, at 1374–76.

technical adjustments,[212] and a machine outputting probabilities cannot replicate them unless the system reconceives proof as a computational threshold rather than a human moral judgment.[213]

C. Inference, Indeterminacy, and the Logic of the Trial

Most trials involve indeterminacy: evidence yields fragments, not certainty.[214] The jury must infer what happened, what was intended, and what was foreseeable,[215] which is why trials are rarely about "facts" in the narrow sense.[216] Even a simple negligence case turns on whether speed was unreasonable, whether risk was perceived, and whether harm was foreseeable—inferential judgments, not observations.[217] Such inference is narrative: jurors draw inferences cohering into an account.[218] Circumstantial evidence is often decisive because intent is inferred from conduct rather than proven by admission, in both criminal law and civil fraud.[219] The trial converts traces of human behavior into conclusions about mental states and responsibility.[220]

AI systems are also inference engines,[221] which seems to align with juries—but misleadingly. AI inference is statistical, drawing on correlations across datasets;[222] jury inference is contextual and

---

[212] *See id.*; *see also Addington*, 441 U.S. at 423–24.
[213] *See* Tribe, *supra* note 191, at 1374–76; Allen & Pardo, *supra* note 178, at 116–21.
[214] *See* 2 John Henry Wigmore, *Evidence in Trials at Common Law* § 2497 (James H. Chadbourn rev. ed. 1979); Laudan, *supra* note 6, at 26–32.
[215] *See* Thayer, *supra* note 9, at 266–68; *See* Restatement (Second) of Torts §§ 281–283, 289–293 (Am. L. Inst. 1965).
[216] *See* Allen & Pardo, *supra* note 178, at 109–16.
[217] *See id.*; Laudan, *supra* note 4, at 35–44.
[218] *See* Pennington & Hastie, *supra* note 197, at 521–27; *See id.* at 525–34.
[219] *Holland v. United States*, 348 U.S. 121, 139–40 (1954); *See Jackson v. Virginia*, 443 U.S. 307, 319 (1979).
[220] *See* Laudan, *supra* note 4, at 44–52.
[221] *See* Trevor Hastie, Robert Tibshirani & Jerome Friedman, *The Elements of Statistical Learning: Data Mining, Inference, and Prediction* 9–18 (2d ed. Springer 2009).
[222] *See id*; Murphy, *supra* note 208, at 1-12.

normative, drawing on lived experience and moral intuition.[223] Those intuitions are not always accurate but are responsive to context in ways statistical models miss.[224] The trial's inferential logic is interpretive, not computational.[225] Indeterminacy also interacts with adversarial structure: lawyers provide curated persuasive narratives, not neutral data.[226] Because AI is vulnerable to input framing,[227] a system treating the record as an objective dataset rather than a contested product of advocacy may be systematically biased by presentation.[228] Litigation is a hostile environment for inference.[229]

D. The "Beyond a Reasonable Doubt" Standard as a Cognitive Constraint

Beyond a reasonable doubt operates as a cognitive constraint designed to induce hesitation, demanding high confidence before punishment.[230] That hesitation is a moral safeguard reflecting that conviction is an act of condemnation backed by force, shaping the juror's whole approach to uncertainty.[231] Courts struggle to define reasonable doubt because its meaning is experiential—a

---

[223] *See* Allen & Pardo, *supra* note 178, at 111–16; *See* Dan M. Kahan, *Culture, Cognition, and Consent: Who Perceives What, and Why, in Acquaintance-Rape Cases,* 158 U. PA. L. REV. 729, 735–41 (2010).
[224] *See* Finale Doshi-Velez & Been Kim, Towards a Rigorous Science of Interpretable Machine Learning 2–5 (2017) (unpublished manuscript), https://arxiv.org/abs/1702.08608.
[225] *See* Allen & Pardo, *supra* note 178, at 116–21.
[226] *See* Lon L. Fuller, The Adversary System, in *Talks on American Law* 34, 38–44; *See* John H. Langbein, *The German Advantage in Civil Procedure*, 52 U. CHI. L. REV. 823, 824–32 (1985).
[227] *See* Ian J. Goodfellow, Jonathon Shlens & Christian Szegedy, Explaining and Harnessing Adversarial Examples, in *International Conference on Learning Representations* (2015), https://arxiv.org/abs/1412.6572.
[228] *See* Battista Biggio & Fabio Roli, *Wild Patterns: Ten Years After the Rise of Adversarial Machine Learning*, 84 PATTERN RECOGNITION 317, 317–24 (2018).
[229] *See id*; Goodfellow et al., *supra* note 227.
[230] *See Winship*, 397 U.S. at 363–64; *See* Fed. Jud. Ctr., *Pattern Criminal Jury Instructions* 17–18 (1987).
[231] *See id.* at 364; *See id.*

felt unease that something does not fit.[232] It is not reducible to an algorithm;[233] the system has never equated it with numerical probability[234] and keeps it deliberately vague to preserve its moral function, restraining conviction when proof feels insufficient even if statistically persuasive.[235]

This vagueness reflects the view that criminal proof is moral, not merely epistemic.[236] Reasonable doubt asks whether the juror can live with the possibility of error—whether the risk of wrongful punishment is acceptable[237]—which is why jurors must be firmly convinced and made to internalize the law's moral asymmetry.[238] AI systems do not experience moral gravity or bear the psychological cost of error.[239] One could require higher thresholds before outputting "guilty," but that is a parameter adjustment, not moral hesitation.[240] The deeper question is whether society would accept a system that convicts without the human experience of doubt;[241] without a mind capable of moral caution, the standard becomes a hollow formula.[242]

III. WHAT AI CAN DO WELL: THE COMPUTATIONAL CASE FOR REPLACEMENT

A. Pattern Recognition and High-Dimensional Evidence

---

[232] *See Victor v. Nebraska*, 511 U.S. 1, 5–17 (1994); *Cage v. Louisiana*, 498 U.S. 39, 40–41 (1990) (per curiam).
[233] *See id.* at 5–17; Ronald J. Allen, *On the Significance of Batting Averages and Strikeout Totals: A Clarification of the "Naked Statistical Evidence" Debate*, 65 TUL. L. REV. 1093, 1110–18 (1991).
[234] *See Victor*, 511 U.S. at 16–17; *see also* Tribe, *supra* note 191, at 1330–35.
[235] *See Victor*, 511 U.S. at 5–6, 16–17; *See Winship*, 397 U.S. at 363–64.
[236] *See id.* at 364; Tribe, *supra* note 191, at 1374–76.
[237] *See Winship*, 397 U.S. at 363–64; *See* 4 Blackstone, *supra* note 201, at *358.
[238] *See* Fed. Jud. Ctr., *supra* note 224, at 17–18; *See Winship*, 397 U.S. at 363–64.
[239] *See* Joshua A. Kroll et al., *Accountable Algorithms*, 165 U. PA. L. REV. 633, 680–87 (2017); Biggio & Roli, *supra* note 228, at 317–24.
[240] *See* Tribe, *supra* note 191, at 1374–76; *See id.*.
[241] *See* Kroll et al., *supra* note 239, at 680–87.
[242] *See Winship*, 397 U.S. at 363–64; *Victor,* 511 U.S. at 5–17.

Modern litigation increasingly involves high-dimensional evidence: surveillance video, location data, transaction histories, digital communications, and forensic science.[243] Such evidence is voluminous and technical, and the jury's limitations become pronounced when jurors must detect patterns across thousands of documents or reconcile many accounts.[244] Scale can overwhelm cognition, pushing jurors toward salient anecdotes.[245] AI, by contrast, is built for high-dimensional analysis: deep learning identifies patterns, classifies images, and detects correlations humans cannot perceive,[246] and could reconstruct timelines, flag anomalous transfers, and surface discrepancies across testimony and records[247]—arguably improving accuracy in complex fraud, mass tort, or conspiracy cases.[248]

This advantage is not trivial.[249] Much criticism of juries rests on their difficulty with technical evidence,[250] and as trials become data-driven the argument for substitution strengthens.[251] AI can at least reduce the cognitive overload that drives reliance on heuristics.[252] But the case must be framed carefully.[253] Pattern recognition is not truth recognition: correlation

---

[243] *See* Fed. R. Evid. 901(a); Orin S. Kerr, *Digital Evidence and the New Criminal Procedure*, 105 COLUM. L. REV. 279, 282–90 (2005).
[244] *See* Maura R. Grossman & Gordon V. Cormack, *Technology-Assisted Review in E-Discovery Can Be More Effective and More Efficient Than Exhaustive Manual Review*, 17 RICH. J.L. & TECH. 11, 11–14 (2011); *See* Vidmar & Hans, *supra* note 168, at 215–48.
[245] *See* Simon, *supra* note 245, at 99–118; *See* Tversky & Kahneman, *supra* note 36, at 1124–31.
[246] *See* Russell & Norvig, *supra* note 19, at 1–10; *See* Trevor Hastie, Robert Tibshirani & Jerome Friedman, *The Elements of Statistical Learning: Data Mining, Inference, and Prediction* 9–18 (2d ed. Springer 2009).
[247] *See* Maura R. Grossman & Gordon V. Cormack, *Technology-Assisted Review in E-Discovery Can Be More Effective and More Efficient Than Exhaustive Manual Review*, 17 RICH. J.L. & TECH. 11, 11–14 (2011); Harry Surden, *Artificial Intelligence and Law: An Overview*, 35 GA. ST. U. L. REV. 1305, 1310–16 (2019).
[248] *See* Vidmar & Hans, *supra* note 168, at 215–48; Surden, *supra* note 5, at 1310–16.
[249] *See* Russell & Norvig, *supra* note 19, at 1–10.
[250] *See* Neil Vidmar & Valerie P. Hans, *supra* note 168, at 215–48.
[251] *See* Surden, *supra* note 5, at 1310–16; *See* Grossman & Cormack, *supra* note 247, at 11–14.
[252] *See* Tversky & Kahneman, *supra* note 36, at 1124–31; Simon, *supra* note 245, at 99–118.
[253] *See* Pasquale, *supra* note 28, at 10–18.

is not causation, anomalies are not misconduct, and patterns may have innocent explanations.[254] The jury's task is to interpret patterns in light of motive, competing narratives, and legal standards.[255] AI's strength is therefore best understood as a tool for evidence management, not a substitute for judgment.[256]

B. Consistency and the Reduction of Human Noise

Juries are criticized for inconsistency: different juries reach different outcomes on similar evidence.[257] Some variability is inevitable,[258] but critics argue that unpredictability makes trials resemble a lottery.[259] AI offers consistency: a system could apply the same framework across cases, eliminating idiosyncratic bias, fatigue, and susceptibility to rhetoric.[260] In principle this could be more equitable where implicit bias plays an outsized role.[261]

But consistency is not justice.[262] A consistent system can consistently err if its assumptions are flawed.[263] And variability is not merely noise: it may reflect legitimate moral disagreement about open-textured concepts like "reasonableness," which juries exist to express.[264] Consistent AI outputs could suppress that democratic pluralism and impose a technocratic standard not

---

[254] *See id.* at 15–18; *See* Pearl, *supra* note 196, at 1–18.
[255] *See* Pennington & Hastie, *supra* note 176, at 525–34.
[256] *See* Surden, *supra* note 5, at 1310–16; Pasquale, *supra* note 28, at 10–18.
[257] *See* Hans & Vidmar, *supra* note 6, at 1–20; Diamond, *supra* note 164, at 717–23.
[258] *See* Devine, *supra* note 176, at 13–60; Hastie, et al., *supra* note 29, at 1 – 15.
[259] *See* Hans & Vidmar, *supra* note 6, at 200–35; Diamond, *supra* note 164, at 717–23.
[260] *See* Surden, *supra* note 5, at 1310 - 16; Pasquale, *supra* note 23, at 19–26.
[261] *See* Jerry Kang et al., *Implicit Bias in the Courtroom*, 59 UCLA L. REV. 1124, 1128–36 (2012); Solon Barocas & Andrew D. Selbst, *Big Data's Disparate Impact*, 104 CALIF. L. REV. 671, 690–712 (2016).
[262] *See* Hart, *supra* note 31, at 124–36.
[263] *See* Pasquale, *supra* note 28, at 10–18.
[264] *See* Sunstein, *supra* note 156, at 71–120; *See* Ronald Dworkin, *Hard Cases*, 88 HARV. L. REV. 1057, 1060–70 (1975).

grounded in community norms.[265] Consistency is valuable only if the criteria are correct;[266] a system trained on historical verdicts may reproduce systemic inequities under the guise of neutrality,[267] making consistency a mechanism of entrenchment.[268] The more consistent the system, the more powerful its errors.[269]

C. Probabilistic Inference and Bayesian Reasoning

AI is fundamentally probabilistic, performing Bayesian-like updating as information arrives.[270] Some scholars argue this suits legal proof, since a fact-finder must determine whether evidence crosses a confidence threshold rather than achieving certainty.[271] Bayesian reasoning promises transparency and rationality, avoiding the documented biases of intuition[272]—biases Kahneman traces to a fast, heuristic "System 1" that deviates predictably from rational-choice models.[273] Predictive-judging research by Katz, Bommarito, and Blackman shows machine-learning models can forecast judicial outcomes with accuracy rivaling experts, revealing that much of adjudication is structured and pattern-dependent enough to be modeled—though the work does

---

[265] *See* Pasquale, *supra* note 28, at 10–18; *see also* Julie E. Cohen, *What Privacy Is For*, 126 HARV. L. REV. 1904, 1934–40 (2013).
[266] *See* Allen & Pardo, *supra* note 178, at 116–21.
[267] *See* Solon Barocas & Andrew D. Selbst, *Big Data's Disparate Impact*, 104 Calif. L. Rev. 671, 690-712 (2016); *see also* Joy Buolamwini & Timnit Gebru, *Gender Shades: Intersectional Accuracy Disparities in Commercial Gender Classification*, 81 PROC. MACH. LEARNING RSCH. 1, 1–15 (2018).
[268] *See* Barocas & Selbst, *supra* note 267, at 716–25; Pasquale, *supra* note 28, at 10–18.
[269] *See* Barocas & Selbst, *supra* note 267, at 716–25; *see also State v. Loomis*, 881 N.W.2d 749, 766–68 (Wis. 2016).Top of Form Bottom of Form.
[270] *See* Murphy, *supra* note 208, at 1–12; Russell & Norvig, *supra* note 19, at 547–60.
[271] *See* Tribe, *supra* note 191, at 1330–35 (1971); Allen & Pardo, *supra* note 178, at 109–16.
[272] *See* Tribe, *supra* note 191, at 1330–35; *see also* Jonathan J. Koehler & Daniel N. Shaviro, *Veridical Verdicts: Increasing Verdict Accuracy Through the Use of Overtly Probabilistic Evidence and Methods*, 75 CORNELL L. REV. 247, 249–55 (1990).
[273] *See* Kahneman, *supra* note 211.

not claim AI "reasons" like a judge and raises its own questions about legitimacy and whether predictive accuracy can substitute for justificatory reasoning.[274]

Yet Bayesian approaches struggle with the reality of trial: priors are contestable, evidence interdependent, credibility hard to quantify, and the law resists reducing burdens to numbers.[275] Probabilistic inference is not normative judgment.[276] Even if AI computed a defendant 92% likely guilty, the law asks whether guilt is proven beyond a reasonable doubt—a standard that cannot be reduced to a probability without changing its meaning.[277] The attraction of probabilistic AI risks redefining proof: asking whether guilt is statistically likely rather than proven, a profound shift in legal epistemology.[278] Probabilistic outputs also create an illusion of precision; a score appears objective but reflects assumptions about model, data, and framing, and grows more dangerous the more "scientific" it appears.[279]

D. Deception Detection, Linguistic Analysis, and Multimodal Models

A provocative argument for substitution is automated credibility assessment.[280] AI can analyze language, tone, and expression, and multimodal models combine text, audio, and video,[281] leading some to imagine AI outperforming poor human lie detectors.[282] But the premise is

---

[274] *See* Murphy, *supra* note 208, at 1–12; Russell & Norvig, *supra* note 19, at 547–60.
[275] *See* Allen & Pardo, *supra* note 178, at 116–21; *See id.*
[276] *See* Hart, *supra* note 31, at 124–36; Tribe, *supra* note 191, at 1374–76.
[277] *See Winship*, 397 U.S. at 363–64; Tribe, *supra* note 191, at 1374–76.
[278] *See* Tribe, *supra* note 191, at 1374–76; *See* Allen & Pardo, *supra* note 178, at 116–21.
[279] *See* Pasquale, *supra* note 23, at 19–26; *See* Barocas & Selbst, supra note 267, at 690–712.
[280] *See generally* Surden, *supra* note 5, at 1312–18.
[281] *See* Mary L. Gray & Siddharth Suri, *Ghost Work: How to Stop Silicon Valley from Building a New Global Underclass* 22–25 (Houghton Mifflin Harcourt 2019); *See generally* Yann LeCun, Yoshua Bengio & Geoffrey Hinton, *Deep Learning*, 521 Nature 436, 438–39 (2015).
[282] *See* John Monahan, *A Jurisprudence of Risk Assessment: Forecasting Harm Among Prisoners, Predators, and Patients*, 92 VA. L. REV. 391, 430–33 (2006); *See* id.

questionable.[283] Deception detection is an uncertain science: some liars are calm and persuasive, some truthful witnesses nervous, and trauma, culture, and neurodivergence distort affect.[284] AI risks treating deviation from a "normative" pattern as dishonesty, encoding bias.[285] Credibility is not reducible to deception: memory is reconstructive and people confabulate, so a deception-focused system might misclassify sincere imperfection as falsehood.[286]

The deeper problem is epistemic.[287] Even accurate deception detection would not resolve what to do with credibility judgments.[288] The law treats credibility as a jury question precisely because it is intertwined with social trust and moral evaluation;[289] replacing it with an algorithmic score shifts authority over trustworthiness from community to machine, raising legitimacy concerns even if the algorithm were better.[290] In *United States v. Scheffer*, the Court upheld a categorical ban on polygraph evidence, emphasizing that determining credibility is a core function of the factfinder that such evidence could usurp—precedent that the Constitution does not require admitting scientific evidence that risks undermining the jury's institutional role.[291]

E. AI Deliberation Through Ensemble and Multi-Agent Architectures

---

283 *See* Richard H. McAdams & Thomas S. Ulen, *Behavioral Criminal Law and Economics*, 74 U. CHI. L. REV. 1, 4–6 (2007).
284 *See* Cary Coglianese & David Lehr, *Regulating by Robot: Administrative Decision Making in the Machine-Learning Era*, 105 GEO. L.J. 1147, 1165–67 (2017); *See* Aldert Vrij, *Detecting Lies and Deceit: Pitfalls and Opportunities* 1–6 (2d ed. Wiley 2008).
285 See Devon Price, *Unmasking Autism: Discovering the New Faces of Neurodiversity* 41–52 (Harmony Books 2022).
286 *See* Barocas & Selbst, *supra* note 267, at 694–703; *See Scheffer*, 523 U.S. at 313.
287 *See generally* Sandra F. Sperino & Suja A. Thomas, *Unequal: How America's Courts Undermine Discrimination Law* 54–60 (Oxford Univ. Press 2017).
288 *See generally* Miranda Fricker, *Epistemic Injustice: Power and the Ethics of Knowing* 1–10 (Oxford Univ. Press 2007).
289 *See id.* at 17–23; *See Scheffer*, 523 U.S. at 313.
290 *See Duncan*, 391 U.S. at 156; *See* Pasquale, *supra* note 23, at 3–9. *See also* Citron, *supra* note 20, at 1301–05.
291 523 U.S. 303 (1998); *Id.*

Designers have proposed mimicking deliberation through ensembles and multi-agent debate: models evaluate evidence and "vote," or agents argue for guilt and innocence before a third weighs them.[292] These mirror the trial's structure[293] and could address the criticism that AI is a single opaque decision-maker, exposing disagreement as uncertainty analogous to a hung jury.[294] But the analogy is fragile.[295] Jurors are genuinely independent minds;[296] AI models are rarely independent, sharing overlapping training data and architecture, so their biases correlate.[297] A "vote" can create an illusion of independent judgment while amplifying shared errors.[298] Deliberation is not aggregation but persuasion and moral confrontation: jurors change their minds from ethical discomfort, which machines do not feel.[299] Multi-agent debate may mimic the *form* of deliberation without its moral substance.[300] Even sophisticated architectures cannot yet replicate the jury's institutional role; they remain tools of plausibility, not institutions of judgment.[301]

IV. THE LIMITS OF MACHINE KNOWLEDGE: AI AS A PLAUSIBILITY ENGINE

---

[292] *See generally* Yarin Gal, Jiri Hron & Alex Kendall, Concrete Dropout, in *Advances in Neural Information Processing Systems 31* 3584, 3584–86; *see also* David Silver et al., *Mastering the Game of Go with Deep Neural Networks and Tree Search*, 529 Nature 484, 484–89 (2016).
[293] *See* Nancy S. Marder, *Deliberations and Disclosures: A Study of Post-Verdict Interviews of Jurors*, 82 IOWA L. REV. 465, 470–76 (1997); *see also* Shari Seidman Diamond & Neil Vidmar, *Jury Room Ruminations on Forbidden Topics*, 87 VA. L. REV. 1857, 1861–66 (2001).
[294] *See* Pasquale, *supra* note 23, at 3–12; *see also* Citron, *supra* note 20, at 1254–56.
[295] *Cf.* Roger C. Park, *Evidence Scholarship Reconsidered: Results of the Interdisciplinary Turn*, 47 B.C. L. REV. 949, 963–67 (2006).
[296] *See Duncan*, 391 U.S. at 156; *see also Witherspoon v. Illinois*, 391 U.S. 510, 519 (1968).
[297] *See* Cynthia Rudin, Stop Explaining Black Box Machine Learning Models for High Stakes Decisions and Use Interpretable Models Instead, 1 *Nature Machine Intelligence* 206, 206–12 (2019); *See* Barocas & Selbst, *supra* note 267, at 686–92.
[298] *See* Kahneman, *supra* note 211, at 201–04; *see also* Cass R. Sunstein, *The Law of Group Polarization*, 10 J. POL. PHIL. 175, 176–79 (2002).
[299] *See* Kalven & Zeisel, *supra* note 164, at 488–92; *See id.*
[300] *See* Searle, *supra* note 56, at 417–21; *see also* Dreyfus, *supra* note 300, at 25–30.
[301] *See United States v. Gaudin*, 515 U.S. 506, 514 (1995); *see also* Laura I. Appleman, *The Plea Jury*, 85 IND. L.J. 731, 739–44 (2010).

A. The Hallucination Problem and the Epistemic Unfitness of Generative Models

The most immediate obstacle is not bias or opacity but the epistemic structure of generative systems: they generate *plausible* outputs, not verified *true* ones.[302] An LLM predicts the next token, so its objective is linguistic coherence, not truth-tracking,[303] which manifests as hallucination—confident falsehoods indistinguishable in tone from correct answers.[304] In adjudication, a system that sometimes invents facts is not merely imperfect but categorically disqualified as fact-finder.[305] The verdict must be the endpoint of disciplined restraint; the jury exists to refuse narrative completion unless proof is sufficient, which is why burdens institutionalize caution.[306] Hallucination reverses that logic, filling gaps rather than admitting uncertainty.[307] Because the costs of legal error are asymmetric and morally charged, a residual error rate tolerable for recommending movies is intolerable when authorizing punishment.[308] This is not a defect patchable by prompting but a structural feature of systems optimized for fluent generation.[309] The trial's error-correction mechanisms—cross-examination, evidentiary rules,

---

302 *See* Pasquale, *supra* note 23, at 3 - 12; *see also* Coglianese & Lehr, *supra* note 284, at 1154–56.
303 *See* Ashish Vaswani et al., Attention Is All You Need, in *Advances in Neural Information Processing Systems 30* 5998, 5998–6008; *see also* Tom B. Brown et al., Language Models Are Few-Shot Learners, in *Advances in Neural Information Processing Systems 33* 1877, 1877–78.
304 *See* Benj Edwards, Why AI Chatbots Are Hallucinating, *Ars Technica* (May 2023), https://arstechnica.com/; *see also* OpenAI, GPT-4 Technical Report 10–12 (2023), https://arxiv.org/abs/2303.08774.
305 *See Winship*, 397 U.S. at 363–64; *see also Addington*, 441 U.S. at 423–24 (1979).
306 *See Winship*, 397 U.S. at 363–64; *see also Jackson v. Virginia*, 443 U.S. 307, 315–16 (1979).
307 *See* OpenAI, GPT-4 Technical Report, *supra* note 304, at 10–12; *See* Surden, *supra* note 5, at 1312–18.
308 *See Addington*, 441 U.S. at 423–24; *see also Santosky v. Kramer*, 455 U.S. 745, 755–56 (1982).
309 *See* OpenAI, GPT-4 Technical Report, *supra* note 304, at 10–12; *see also* Bender et al., *supra* note 44, at 615–18.

appellate review—presume a fact-finder trying to *avoid* invention;[310] one that fabricates does not fit that architecture.[311] Hallucination collides directly with the commitments distinguishing proof from storytelling.[312]

B. The Frame Problem and Relevance Determination

Even if hallucination were solved, relevance would remain.[313] Trials are about determining what *matters*, not processing all information.[314] The adversarial system is a relevance engine relying on the fact-finder to decide which facts are salient.[315] The "frame problem" in AI captures the difficulty of deciding what is relevant in an open-ended world;[316] humans solve it through embodied experience, while AI can process everything yet fail to identify what matters.[317] This is acute in law, where relevance differs from common sense: evidence may be excluded as prejudicial or be technically relevant yet distorting.[318] Jurors make relevance calls within the admissible set—what to emphasize, discount, or treat as decisive—using tacit knowledge about motive and

---

[310] *See Crawford v. Washington*, 541 U.S. 36, 61–62 (2004); *see also Daubert v. Merrell Dow Pharm., Inc.*, 509 U.S. 579, 592–95 (1993).
[311] *See Crawford*, 541 U.S. at 61–62; *see also Daubert*, 509 U.S. at 590.
[312] *See Winship*, 397 U.S. at 363–64; *see also* Jerome Frank, *Are Judges Human*?, 80 U. PA. L. REV. 17, 20–24 (1931).
[313] *See* Bender et al., *supra* note 44, at 615–18; *see also* OpenAI, GPT-4 Technical Report, *supra* note 304, at 10–12.
[314] *See* Fed. R. Evid. 401 advisory committee's note (1972); *see also* 1 Kenneth S. Broun et al., *McCormick on Evidence* § 185.
[315] *See* Mirjan R. Damaška, *The Faces of Justice and State Authority* 138–41 (Yale Univ. Press 1986); *see also* Lon L. Fuller, *The Forms and Limits of Adjudication*, 92 HARV. L. REV. 353, 382–86 (1978).
[316] *See* John McCarthy & Patrick J. Hayes, Some Philosophical Problems from the Standpoint of Artificial Intelligence, in *Machine Intelligence 4* 463, 463–502; *see also* Daniel C. Dennett, Cognitive Wheels: The Frame Problem of AI, in *Minds, Machines and Evolution* 129, 129–51.
[317] *See* Dreyfus, *supra* note 300, at 13–19; *see also* Maurice Merleau-Ponty, *Phenomenology of Perception* 79–83 (1945).
[318] *See* Fed. R. Evid. 401; *see also Old Chief v. United States*, 519 U.S. 172, 179–80 (1997).

ordinary causation.[319] A machine could model relevance statistically, but the law cannot accept relevance defined as correlation with past verdicts, which would convert proof evaluation into outcome prediction.[320] The frame problem thus converges with circularity: an AI learning relevance from prior verdicts may learn the *style* of past decision-making rather than the normative structure of proof.[321]

C. The Black Box Problem and the Limits of Explainability

AI opacity presents another mismatch.[322] Even where systems produce impressive results, they often cannot explain how faithfully;[323] "explainable AI" often yields post hoc narratives that satisfy expectations rather than reveal the decision procedure.[324] This matters because adjudication is about justification under public rules, not merely outcomes.[325] Jury verdicts are themselves often

---

[319] *See Tanner v. United States*, 483 U.S. 107, 127 (1987); *see also United States v. Gaudin*, 515 U.S. 506, 514 (1995).
[320] *See* Kleinberg et al, *supra* note 298, at 120–28; see also Barocas & Selbst, *supra* note 267, at 685–92.
[321] *See* McCarthy & Hayes, *supra* note 316, at 463–502; *see also* Danielle Keats Citron, *Technological Due Process*, 85 WASH. U. L. REV. 1249, 1301–05 (2008).
[322] *See* Jenna Burrell, How the Machine "Thinks": Understanding Opacity in Machine Learning Algorithms, 3 *Big Data & Soc'y* 1, 1–6 (2016); *see also* Pasquale, *supra* note 23, at 3–12.
[323] *See* Cynthia Rudin, Stop Explaining Black Box Machine Learning Models for High Stakes Decisions and Use Interpretable Models Instead, 1 *Nature Machine Intelligence* 206, 206–12 (2019); *see also* Finale Doshi-Velez & Been Kim, Towards a Rigorous Science of Interpretable Machine Learning 1–7 (2017) (unpublished manuscript), https://arxiv.org/abs/1702.08608.
[324] *See* Zachary C. Lipton, The Mythos of Model Interpretability, in *ICML Workshop on Human Interpretability in Machine Learning* 1, 2–6 (2016), https://arxiv.org/abs/1606.03490; *see also* Sandra Wachter, Brent Mittelstadt & Chris Russell, *Counterfactual Explanations Without Opening the Black Box: Automated Decisions and the GDPR*, 31 HARV. J.L. & TECH. 841, 846–53 (2018).
[325] *See* Lon L. Fuller, *The Forms and Limits of Adjudication*, 92 HARV. L. REV. 353, 364–70 (1978); *see also* Jerry L. Mashaw, *Reasoned Administration: The European Union, the United States, and the Project of Democratic Governance*, 76 GEO. WASH. L. REV. 99, 104–10 (2007).

unreasoned,[326] but juries are not black boxes in the same way:[327] their legitimacy rests on transparent procedure—public testimony, public argument, citizen deliberation—and the *type* of reasoning is human and democratic.[328] AI opacity is not privacy but unintelligibility, often uninterpretable even when disclosed.[329] AI fact-finding would shift trust from citizens to engineers, asking the system to accept that an opaque process reached the right answer,[330] which erodes legitimacy: a machine verdict would be contested as procedurally illegitimate because its reasons cannot be articulated in the language of law and moral responsibility.[331]

D. Adversarial Manipulation and the Weaponization of Litigation Strategy

Litigation is not neutral but adversarial, designed to reward strategic behavior, so any system central to verdicts becomes a target.[332] Machine learning is vulnerable to adversarial attacks in which small input perturbations induce large output changes;[333] annoying in consumer contexts, in trials these would become strategy,[334] with parties crafting presentation and witness

---

[326] *See* Kleinberg et al, *supra* note 298, at 120–28; *see also* Barocas & Selbst, *supra* note 267, at 685–92.

[327] *See Winship*, 397 U.S. at 363–64; *see also Jackson*, 443 U.S. at 315–16.

[328] *See* Citron, *supra* note 20, at 1301–05; *see also* Barocas & Selbst, *supra* note 267, at 694–703.

[329] *See* Doshi-Velez & Kim, *supra* note 224, at 1–6 (unpublished manuscript); *see also* Rudin, *supra* note 297 at 206–12.

[330] *See* John Rawls, *A Theory of Justice* 136–42 (rev. ed. 1999); *see also* Habermas, *supra* note 326, at 107 – 10.

[331] *See* Fed. R. Civ. P. 49; *see also United States v. Powell*, 469 U.S. 57, 66 (1984).

[332] *See* Fuller, *supra* note 315, at 382–86; *see also* Damaška, *supra* note 315, at 138–41.

[333] *See* Ian J. Goodfellow, Jonathon Shlens & Christian Szegedy, Explaining and Harnessing Adversarial Examples (2015) (unpublished manuscript), https://arxiv.org/abs/1412.6572; *see also* Aleksander Madry et al., Towards Deep Learning Models Resistant to Adversarial Attacks, in *International Conference on Learning Representations* 1, 1–4 (2018), https://arxiv.org/abs/1706.06083.

[334] *See* Goodfellow et al., *supra* note 333, at 1–4; *see also* Nicholas Carlini & David Wagner, Towards Evaluating the Robustness of Neural Networks, in *2017 IEEE Symposium on Security and Privacy* 39, 39–57 (IEEE 2017).

preparation to exploit model sensitivities.[335] This differs qualitatively from jury persuasion: jurors are heterogeneous, socially grounded, and able to resist through deliberation, whereas a model may be systematically susceptible to input engineering exploitable at scale.[336] Litigation would become a contest over who can best "prompt" or "poison" the fact-finder rather than prove the truth.[337] Because models can be patched and tuned, adversarial behavior creates a moving target complicating due process—defendants judged by a changing model, plaintiffs alleging exploited vulnerabilities, courts unable to tell evidence from exploitation.[338] The structure of trial would become an attack surface.[339]

E. AI as a Plausibility Engine: Why "Sounds Right" Cannot Equal "Is True"

The unifying problem is that LLMs are plausibility engines: their outputs are optimized to look like good reasoning, not to be it.[340] This is dangerous because trials are already narrative contests in which lawyers trade in plausibility, and the jury's task is to treat plausibility as insufficient and demand proof.[341] AI especially good at producing plausible accounts risks collapsing the distinction between persuasion and proof that the trial exists to preserve.[342] This is

---

[335] *See* Coglianese & Lehr, *supra* note 284, at 1171–74; *see also* Madry et al., *supra* note 333, at 1–4.
[336] *See* Jerry L. Mashaw, *Reasoned Administration: The European Union, the United States, and the Project of Democratic Governance*, 76 GEO. WASH. L. REV. 99, 104–10 (2007); *see also* Habermas, *supra* note 326, at 107–10.
[337] *See* Pasquale, *supra* note 23, at 8–12; *see also* Citron, *supra* note 20, at 1301–05.
[338] *See* Citron, *supra* note 20, at 1301–05; *see also* Cary Coglianese & David Lehr, Transparency and Algorithmic Governance, in *Administrative Law from the Inside Out* 319, 330–33.
[339] *See* Pasquale, *supra* note 23, at 8–12; *see also* Papernot et al., *supra* note 337, at 506–19.
[340] *See generally* Tarek R. Besold et al., Neural-Symbolic Learning and Reasoning: A Survey and Interpretation, 7 *Frontiers in Artificial Intelligence* 1 (2021); *see also* Jason Wei et al., Chain-of-Thought Prompting Elicits Reasoning in Large Language Models, in *Advances in Neural Information Processing Systems 35* 24824, 24824–37.
[341] *See generally* Bennett L. Gershman, *The New Prosecutors*, 53 U. PITT. L. REV. 393, 431–34 (1992); *see also* Nancy Pennington & Reid Hastie, supra note 117, at 242–46.
[342] *See* Fed. R. Evid. 401–403; *see also Daubert,* 509 U.S. at 589–95.

why replacement differs from assistance.[343] AI excels at summarizing and cross-referencing evidence, where plausibility is not the final criterion;[344] but a fact-finder must decide whether a narrative is warranted given admissible evidence and legal thresholds.[345] Until AI can reliably refuse completion—say "the evidence does not justify an answer" rather than produce a best guess—its central strength remains a liability in adjudication.[346]

V. CREDIBILITY AND THE "HUMAN" DIMENSION OF TESTIMONY

A. Memory, Confabulation, and the Nonlinear Nature of Truth

Testimony depends on memory, and memory is not a recording device but reconstructive: people reassemble fragments and fill gaps without awareness.[347] So sincere witnesses can be wrong and inconsistent witnesses truthful; a fact-finder must evaluate testimony not as truth-versus-deception but as a complex artifact of cognition.[348] This is what makes credibility hard to automate.[349] A system treating inconsistency as falsity will be wrong for human reasons, since discrepancies reflect normal memory decay, stress, trauma, and the distortion of peripheral

---

[343] *See generally* Coglianese & Lehr, *supra* note 284, at 1162–66; *see also* U.S. Dep't of Com., Nat'l Inst. of Standards & Tech., *Artificial Intelligence Risk Management Framework (AI RMF 1.0)* 4–7 (2023), https://nvlpubs.nist.gov/nistpubs/ai/NIST.AI.100-1.pdf.

[344] *See generally* Daniel N. Kluttz & Deirdre K. Mulligan, *Automated Decision Support Technologies and the Legal Profession*, 34 BERKELEY TECH. L.J. 853, 864–70 (2019); *see also* Maura R. Grossman & Gordon V. Cormack, *Technology-Assisted Review in E-Discovery Can Be More Effective and More Efficient Than Exhaustive Manual Review*, 17 RICH. J.L. & TECH. 11, ¶¶ 2–4 (2011).

[345] *See Old Chief*, 519 U.S. at 187–89; *see also* Pennington & Hastie, *supra* note 176, at 242–46.

[346] See Bender et al., *supra* note 44, at 615–17; *see also* OpenAI, GPT-4 Technical Report, *supra* note 304, at 11–12.

[347] See 3A John Henry Wigmore, *Evidence in Trials at Common Law* § 874, at 259–60; *see also* Fed. R. Evid. 602.

[348] *See United States v. Wade*, 388 U.S. 218, 228 (1967); *see also Neil v. Biggers*, 409 U.S. 188, 199–200 (1972).

[349] *See generally* John Monahan & Jennifer L. Skeem, *Risk Assessment in Criminal Sentencing*, 12 Ann. Rev. Clinical Psych. 489, 500–06 (2016); *see also* Sandra G. Mayson, *Bias In, Bias Out*, 128 YALE L.J. 2218, 2227–33 (2019).

details.[350] Jurors intuitively understand these dynamics because they have lived them—knowing people misremember without lying, which is part of why the jury is entrusted with credibility.[351] An AI scoring credibility by linguistic coherence would punish the very irregularities characteristic of human memory, over-crediting polished narratives and under-crediting messy ones,[352] inverting the proper posture: skepticism toward smoothness, sensitivity toward imperfection.[353] It would reward performance rather than truth.[354]

B. Trauma, Demeanor, and the Misreading of Human Behavior

Credibility assessment also involves demeanor.[355] Courts historically treat it as relevant,[356] but it is a notoriously unreliable indicator of truthfulness: people display stress for many reasons, some liars are calm, and trauma, neurodivergence, and cultural difference alter affect, cadence, and eye contact.[357] Lay observers often mistake "normal" affect for sincerity.[358] If demeanor is unreliable for humans, it is more dangerous for machines: a multimodal model could encode and amplify the demeanor fallacy, treating deviation from a learned norm as deception,[359] and because

---

350 *See* Kassin et al., *supra* note 283 at 405–16; *see also Scheffer*, 523 U.S. at 313.
351 *See* Hans & Vidmar, *supra* note 6, at 11–16; *see also* Hastie, et al., *supra* note 29, at 22–28.
352 *See* Margaret Mitchell et al., Model Cards for Model Reporting, in *Proceedings of the 2019 ACM Conference on Fairness, Accountability, and Transparency* 220, 221–25 (Assoc. Comput. Mach. 2019); *see also* Bender et al., *supra* note 44, at 615–17.
353 *See* Kahneman, *supra* note 211, at 199–204; *see also* Fed. R. Evid. 403.
354 *See Scheffer*, 523 U.S. at 313; *see also* Harry Surden, *Machine Learning and Law*, 89 WASH. L. REV. 87, 99–107 (2014).
355 *See* 3A Wigmore, *supra* note 347, at § 946, at 778–81; *see also* Olin Guy Wellborn III, *Demeanor*, 76 CORNELL L. REV. 1075, 1078–80 (1991).
356 *See Mattox v. United States*, 156 U.S. 237, 242–43 (1895); *see also Anderson v. City of Bessemer City*, 470 U.S. 564, 575 (1985).
357 *See* Wellborn, *supra* note 276, at 1075–77; *see also* Jeremy A. Blumenthal, *A Wipe of the Hands, a Lick of the Lips: The Validity of Demeanor Evidence in Assessing Witness Credibility*, 72 NEB. L. REV. 1157, 1160–66 (1993).
358 *See* Sheri Lynn Johnson, *Cross-Racial Identification Errors in Criminal Cases*, 69 CORNELL L. REV. 934, 939–45 (1984); *see also* Wellborn, *supra* note 276, at 1083–89.
359 *See Scheffer*, 523 U.S. at 312–13; *see also* Christopher Slobogin, *The Civilization of the Criminal Law*, 58 VAND. L. REV. 121, 167–70 (2005).

AI outputs appear objective the bias is harder to challenge—an impression can be cross-examined, a "deception score" appears scientific.[360] The stakes fall unevenly: marginalized speakers, trauma survivors, non-native speakers, and neurodivergent individuals are most likely to be misread, so automated credibility risks institutionalizing misinterpretation where trustworthiness matters most.[361]

C. Cultural Linguistics and the Risk of Automated Credibility Bias

Language is culturally situated: people narrate differently by dialect, education, and norms, valuing directness or indirection, hedging from politeness, or emphasizing context over chronology.[362] These differences affect how persuasive testimony sounds.[363] Human jurors may misread them; AI trained on dominant patterns may misread them at scale.[364] The problem operates through seemingly neutral features—grammar, syntax, pace—so a model associating patterns with "truthfulness" learns proxies for class, register, and education, effectively treating "speaks like the training data" as "credible."[365] That is corrosive to legitimacy, shifting credibility from contextual judgment to a conformity metric.[366] The system has long struggled to keep credibility from

---

[360] *See* Burrell, *supra* note 322, at 1 - 5; *see also* Pasquale, *supra* note 23, at 3–9.
[361] *See* Sonja B. Starr, *Evidence-Based Sentencing and the Scientific Rationalization of Discrimination*, 66 STAN. L. REV. 803, 806–15 (2014); *See* Joy Buolamwini & Timnit Gebru, Gender Shades: Intersectional Accuracy Disparities in Commercial Gender Classification, in *Proceedings of Machine Learning Research* vol. 81, 1, 1–15.
[362] *See* Pierre Bourdieu, *Language and Symbolic Power* 37–39 (John B.); *see also* Susan U. Phillips, *Ideology in the Language of Judges: How Judges Practice Law, Politics, and Courtroom Control* 16–19 (Oxford Univ. Press 1998).
[363] *See* Susan Berk-Seligson, *The Bilingual Courtroom: Court Interpreters in the Judicial Process* 59–64; *see also* Seidman Diamond & Jessica M. Salerno, *Empirical Analysis of Jury Decision Making*, 50 ARIZ. ST. L.J. 437, 453–58 (2018).
[364] *See* Sheri Lynn Johnson, *Cross-Racial Identification Errors in Criminal Cases*, 69 CORNELL L. REV. 934, 939–45 (1984); *see also* Wellborn, *supra* note 276, at 1083–89.
[365] *See* Charles R. Lawrence III, *The Id, the Ego, and Equal Protection: Reckoning with Unconscious Racism,* 39 STAN. L. REV. 317, 322–28 (1987); *see also* Kang et al., *supra* note 261, at 1129–35.
[366] *See* Citron, *supra* note 20, at 1267–75; *see also* Pasquale, *supra* note 23, at 3–9.

collapsing into class and culture judgments, with instructions focusing jurors on perception and bias rather than mannerisms;[367] an AI system would do the opposite, turning mannerisms into dispositive data.[368] Credibility, even imperfectly assessed, remains among the strongest arguments against substitution: the function is deeply human, socially embedded, and resistant to formalization.[369]

D. The Jury's "Common Sense" as Embodied Knowledge

Jurors are instructed to use "common sense."[370] Vague as it sounds, it captures jurors' embodied understanding of how people behave, how accidents happen, how fear manifests, and how motives operate[371]—an experiential lens, not a dataset, that lets them evaluate plausibility socially: does this story comport with ordinary human behavior?[372] Work on embodied cognition argues human concepts are rooted in bodily experience;[373] even setting aside strong versions, the jury's interpretive competence depends on experiential grounding current AI lacks.[374] AI can mimic common-sense language because it appears in text, but mimicry is not possession: a model

---

[367] *See* Deborah W. Denno, *Perspective on Bias in the Criminal Justice System*, 70 EMORY L.J. 803, 809–16 (2021); *see also* Lawrence, *supra* note 365, at 322–28.

[368] *See* Andrea Roth, *Machine Testimony*, 126 YALE L.J. 1972, 1982–90 (2017); *see also* *Scheffer*, 523 U.S. at 312–13.

[369] *See Scheffer*, 523 U.S. at 313; *see also* Surden, *supra* note 5, at 99–107.

[370] *See* 1A Kevin F. O'Malley, et al, *supra* note 92 at § 15:01; *see also* 3A Wigmore, *supra* note 347, at § 875, at 265–70.

[371] *See* Hans & Vidmar, *supra* note 6, at 11–16; *see also* Hastie, et al., *supra* note 29, at 22–28.

[372] *See* George Lakoff & Mark Johnson, *Philosophy in the Flesh: The Embodied Mind and Its Challenge to Western Thought* 3–7 (Basic Books 1999); *see also* Maurice Merleau-Ponty, *Phenomenology of Perception* 203–06 (1945).

[373] *See* Lakoff & Johnson, *supra* note 372, at 3–7; *see also* Andy Clark, *Being There: Putting Brain, Body, and World Together Again* 1–9 (MIT Press 1997).

[374] *See* Surden, *supra* note 5, at 99–107; *see also* John Monahan & Jennifer L. Skeem, Risk Assessment in Criminal Sentencing, 12 *Ann. Rev. Clinical Psych.* 489, 500–06 (2016).

can produce a sentence about what "people usually do" without any worldly anchor.[375] That gap matters most in the gray areas where law operates, where facts are uncertain and moral judgment is required.[376] Credibility and testimony are the hard core of the substitution problem: trials turn not on data abundance but on human ambiguity, which the jury copes with through collective, embodied judgment.[377] AI can organize evidence and highlight inconsistencies but cannot replicate the grounded interpretive competence credibility demands.[378]

VI. THE NORMATIVE AND MORAL STRUCTURE OF FACT-FINDING

A. Negligence, Reasonableness, and Community Standards

Negligence illustrates the core difficulty: much of what juries "find" is evaluative, not descriptive.[379] The standard asks whether the defendant acted as a "reasonable person" would—not a measurement of what happened but a judgment about what should have happened, an institutionalized moral assessment delegated to the jury because it reflects community norms.[380] The "reasonable person" is a civic construct shaped by expectations of prudence and responsibility.[381] This is why juries, not judges alone, decide reasonableness: it is open-textured

---

[375] *See* Bender et al., *supra* note 44, at 615–17; *see also* Luciano Floridi & Massimo Chiriatti, GPT-3: Its Nature, Scope, Limits, and Consequences, 40 *Minds & Machines* 681, 684–88 (2020).
[376] *See* Dan M. Kahan, *The Supreme Court 2010 Term—Foreword: Neutral Principles, Motivated Cognition, and Some Problems for Constitutional Law*, 125 HARV. L. REV. 1, 18–25 (2011); *see also* Dworkin, *supra* note 265, at 1057–63.
[377] *See Scheffer*, 523 U.S. at 313; *see also* Wellborn, *supra* note 276, at 1078–80.
[378] *See* Surden, *supra* note 5, at 99–107; *see also* Roth, *supra* note 361, at 1982–90.
[379] *See* Kahan, *supra* note 376, at 18–25; *see also* Dworkin, *supra* note 265, at 1057–63.
[380] *See* Restatement (Second) of Torts § 283 (Am. L. Inst. 1965); *see also* W. Page Keeton et al., *Prosser and Keeton on the Law of Torts* § 32, at 173–74.
[381] *See* Restatement (Second) of Torts § 283 cmt. c (Am. L. Inst. 1965); *see also* Prosser & Keeton, *supra* note 380, § 32, at 174–75.

and must adapt to changing conditions and technologies.[382] What was reasonable in 1950 may be reckless in 2026, and urban may differ from rural; the jury updates the legal system's normative expectations and supplies the social meaning law requires.[383]

AI can model behavior, predicting what most drivers or employers do,[384] but predicting behavior is not prescribing it.[385] A system trained on human behavior may reproduce human carelessness: that most people text while driving does not make it reasonable.[386] Reasonableness is a normative standard, not an empirical average; the jury decides what is acceptable, not what is typical—a distinction fatal to the claim that AI can substitute by modeling patterns.[387] The standard also reflects the jury's role as democratic interpreter: a negligence verdict communicates a social judgment about conduct, affirming norms of caution in a way that shapes behavior.[388] A machine verdict may allocate damages efficiently but cannot perform that civic function of communal moral pronouncement, which is why negligence is a window into why jury fact-finding is inseparable from democratic legitimacy.[389]

B. Intent, Motive, and the Irreducibility of Mental State Inference

Criminal and many civil claims require juries to determine mental states—intent, knowledge, recklessness, malice.[390] These are inferred from behavior and circumstance, but the inference is

---

382 *See Markman v. Westview Instruments, Inc.,* 517 U.S. 370, 377 (1996); *see also* 57A Am. Jur. 2d Negligence § 956 (2026).
383 *See The T.J. Hooper*, 60 F.2d 737, 740 (2d Cir. 1932) (Hand, J.); *see also* Restatement (Third) of Torts: Liab. for Physical & Emotional Harm § 13 cmt. d (Am. L. Inst. 2010).
384 *See* Surden, *supra* note 5, at 92–99; *See id.* at 99–107.
385 *See* Surden, *supra* note 5, at 92–99; *see also* Pasquale, *supra* note 23, at 3–9.
386 *See* Barocas & Selbst, *supra* note 267, at 691–95; *see also* Mayson, *supra* note 268, at 2227–33.
387 *See* Restatement (Second) of Torts § 283 cmt. b (Am. L. Inst. 1965); *see also* Holmes, *supra* note 381, at 108–11.
388 *See* Amar, *supra* note 8, at 1183–87; *see also* Kalven & Zeisel, *supra* note 164, at 8–12.
389 *See* Citron, *supra* note 20, at 1267–75; *see also* Pasquale, *supra* note 23, at 3–9.
390 *See* Model Penal Code § 2.02(2) (Am. L. Inst. 1962); *see also* 18 U.S.C. § 1030(a) (2022).

interpretive, requiring human understanding of motive, fear, impulse, and rationalization.[391] Mental state inference is among the most human aspects of fact-finding: the jury decides not merely what happened but what kind of person the defendant was being.[392] AI might seem capable, classifying sentiment and modeling decisions,[393] but legal mental state inference is about moral attribution, not statistical likelihood.[394] To say someone acted "intentionally" assigns responsibility at the highest level;[395] the law uses intent as a moral sorting mechanism distinguishing accident, negligence, recklessness, and malice by blameworthiness, not just probability.[396]

A machine might estimate that conduct is consistent with intentional wrongdoing, but the law does not ask juries to estimate consistency; it asks whether the state has proven intent beyond a reasonable doubt—a moral decision about whether jurors will label the defendant as having chosen wrongdoing, carrying weight because it is tied to punishment.[397] A machine can output a label but cannot experience the ethical seriousness of labeling a human being as intentionally criminal.[398] Motive adds complexity: often relevant, usually ambiguous, since people act for multiple and unconscious reasons and rationalize themselves.[399] Juries interpret motive with

---

[391] *See Morissette v. United States*, 342 U.S. 246, 274 (1952).
[392] *See* Henry M. Hart, Jr., The Aims of the Criminal Law, 23 *Law & Contemp. Probs.* 401, 404–06 (1958); *see also* Model Penal Code § 1.02(1)(a) (Am. L. Inst. 1962).
[393] *See* Surden, *supra* note 5, at 92–99.
[394] *See Morissette*, 342 U.S. at 274; *see also* Hart, *supra* note 389, at 404–06.
[395] *See* Hart, *supra* note 389, at 404–06; *see also Morissette*, 342 U.S. at 250–52.
[396] *See Morissette*, 342 U.S. at 250–52; *see also* Kenneth W. Simons, *Rethinking Mental States*, 72 B.U. L. REV. 463, 468–76 (1992).
[397] *See Winship*, 397 U.S. at 363–64; *see also* Paul H. Robinson, *Structure and Function in Criminal Law* 12–18 (Oxford Univ. Press 1997).
[398] *See* id. *See also* Searle, *supra* note 56, at 417–24; *see also* Citron, *supra* note 20, at 1267–75.
[399] *See* Fed. R. Evid. 404(b)(2); *see also* 1A O'Malley et al., *supra* note 92, § 15:05.

intuitive appreciation for this ambiguity;[400] AI risks reducing motive to proxies—socioeconomic markers, affiliations, stereotypes—transforming a moral inquiry into crude classification.[401]

C. Proximate Cause as a Moral Judgment

Proximate cause is the clearest example that fact-finding is not merely descriptive. It concerns moral responsibility, not physical causation:[402] the law draws a line between causes "too remote" and those justifying liability, a normative boundary reflecting fairness and foreseeability rather than physics.[403] Foreseeability itself is moralized, asking what risks a person should have considered.[404] This is why proximate cause resists formalization and courts treat it as a question of judgment[405]—the law's way of saying that contribution to a causal chain does not entail responsibility for all that followed.[406] AI can build causal graphs, but proximate cause is about deciding which causal links matter legally, which depends on community intuitions about fairness and blame.[407] Replacing juries here would force the law to redefine proximate cause as a statistical rather than a fairness concept, converting a moral doctrine into a predictive algorithm—more consistent but less human.[408]

D. The Jury as a Responsibility-Allocation Institution

---

[400] *See* Hans & Vidmar, *supra* note 6, at 11–16; *see also* Hastie et al., *supra* note 29, at 22–28.
[401] *See* Barocas & Selbst, *supra* note 267, at 691–95; *see also* Mayson, *supra* note 268, at 2227–33. *See* Barocas & Selbst, *supra* note 267, at 691–95.
[402] *See* Prosser & Keeton, *supra* note 380, § 41, at 264–65. *See* Restatement (Third) of Torts: Liab. for Physical & Emotional Harm § 29 (Am. L. Inst. 2010); *see also* Restatement (Second) of Torts § 431 (Am. L. Inst. 1965).
[403] *See Palsgraf,* 162 N.E. at 103–04; *see also Exxon Co. v. Sofec, Inc.,* 517 U.S. 830, 837–39 (1996).
[404] *See* Restatement (Third) of Torts: Liab. for Physical & Emotional Harm § 29 cmt. b (Am. L. Inst. 2010); *see also* Green, *supra* note 404, at 562–67.
[405] *See* Tribe, *supra* note 191, at 1330–36; *see also* Citron, *supra* note 20, at 1267–75.
[406] *See Derdiarian v. Felix Contracting Corp.,* 414 N.E.2d 666, 670–71 (N.Y. 1980); *see also* Restatement (Second) of Torts § 440 (Am. L. Inst. 1965) (defining superseding cause).
[407] *See Exxon*, 517 U.S. at 838–39; *see also* Prosser & Keeton, *supra* note 380, § 41, at 264–68.
[408] *See* Tribe, *supra* note 191, at 1330–36; *see also* Citron, *supra* note 20, at 1267–75.

These doctrines reveal that the jury is not simply a truth-finding body but a responsibility-allocation institution deciding who should bear the consequences.[409] This is why verdicts feel different from administrative determinations: they are moral pronouncements embodying the community's authority to condemn, excuse, or punish.[410] That function is inseparable from legitimacy—society accepts imprisonment or damages not merely because evidence was processed but because citizens participated in a ritual of accountability that makes the community complicit in coercive power and thereby legitimizes it.[411] Without that ritual, adjudication risks appearing as bureaucratic force.[412] AI cannot replicate this: even if it replicated accuracy, it cannot replicate accountability.[413] A machine cannot be morally responsible, blamed for wrongful conviction, or feel regret;[414] its verdict would be a technical output rather than a communal moral conclusion—a foundational difference.[415] This is why the jury persists despite its inefficiencies: not because laypeople are superior statisticians but because coercion requires legitimacy grounded in human responsibility.[416]

VII. TOWARD AN AI "JURY": THEORETICAL ARCHITECTURES AND FAILURES

A. An AI Fact-Finder Built on Probabilistic Models

---

[409] *See* William M. Landes & Richard A. Posner, *The Private Enforcement of Law*, 4 J. LEGAL STUD. 1, 33–36 (1975); *see also* Kalven & Zeisel, *supra* note 164, at 3–12.
[410] *See* Jerry L. Mashaw, *Bureaucratic Justice: Managing Social Security Disability Claims* 23–29 (Yale Univ. Press 1983); *see also* Paul R. Verkuil, *The Emerging Concept of Administrative Procedure*, 78 COLUM. L. REV. 258, 259–63 (1978).
[411] *See Duncan*, 391 U.S. at 156; *see also* Alexis de Tocqueville, *Democracy in America* 270–72.
[412] *See* Jerry L. Mashaw, Prodelegation: Why Administrators Should Make Political Decisions, 1 *J.L. Econ. & Org.* 81, 82–89 (1985); *see also* Citron, *supra* note 20, at 1267–75.
[413] *See* Citron, *supra* note 20, at 1267–75; *see also* Pasquale, *supra* note 23, at 3–9.
[414] *See* Searle, *supra* note 56, at 417–24; *see also* Luciano Floridi, *The Ethics of Information* 78–83 (Oxford Univ. Press 2013).
[415] *See* Floridi, *supra* note 414, at 78–83; *see also* Citron, *supra* note 20, at 1267–75.
[416] *See Duncan*, 391 U.S. at 155–56; *see also* de Tocqueville, *supra* note 142, at 270–72.

One architecture is a probabilistic fact-finder outputting likelihood estimates for competing propositions, updating as evidence arrives and incorporating burdens by requiring a threshold before convicting.[417] Its appeal is that it aligns adjudication with rational inference, replacing intuitive narrative with explicit calculation.[418] But the appeal misleads: legal proof is not merely probability, and burdens are not numeric.[419] Courts resist equating reasonable doubt with a probability threshold because the standard is moral, designed to produce hesitation.[420] A probabilistic AI jury would either fail to comply with legal standards or force the system to redefine them computationally.[421] Such models also require priors—exactly what litigation contests, since parties disagree about the significance of evidence.[422] A system encoding priors encodes normative choices, raising the question of who decides them—legislature, judiciary, or vendor—each answer shifting adjudication toward centralized technocratic control.[423]

B. The Multi-Model "Synthetic Jury" Approach

A second architecture is the synthetic jury: multiple independently trained models producing assessments aggregated by voting, meant to mirror collective error-filtering.[424] But independence is illusory: models trained on similar data with similar architectures share correlated

---

417 *See* Tribe, *supra* note 191, at 1330–36; *see also* Ronald J. Allen, *A Reconceptualization of Civil Trials*, 66 B.U. L. REV. 401, 404–10 (1986).
418 *See* Tribe, *supra* note 191, at 1330–36; *see also* Finkelstein & Fairley, *supra* note 418, at 489–503.
419 *See* Tribe, *supra* note 191, at 1330–36; *See Addington*, 441 U.S. at 423–24.
420 *See Victor v. Nebraska*, 511 U.S. 1, 5 (1994); *see also Winship*, 397 U.S. at 363–64.
421 *See* Tribe, *supra* note 191, at 1330–36; *see also* Allen & Leiter, *supra* note 12, at 1497–1504.
422 *See* Pearl, *supra* note 196, at 1–7; *see also* Allen & Leiter, *supra* note 12, at 1497–1504.
423 *See* Tribe, *supra* note 191, at 1330–36; *see also* Cass R. Sunstein, *The Cost-Benefit State: The Future of Regulatory Protection* 8–14.
424 *See* Ian Goodfellow, Yoshua Bengio & Aaron Courville, *Deep Learning* 417–23 (MIT Press 2016); *see also* Rich Caruana et al., Ensemble Selection from Libraries of Models, in *Proceedings of the Twenty-First International Conference on Machine Learning* 18, 18–26 (Assoc. Comput. Mach. 2004).

biases, so their errors cluster and the appearance of deliberation conceals systemic distortion—confident convergence on the wrong answer from shared blind spots.[425] A synthetic jury also cannot replicate deliberation's moral dynamics: human jurors persuade through moral discomfort, empathy, and lived experience, changing votes from doubt about condemning another person.[426] AI experiences no such pressure; its "deliberation" is computation, producing the form of disagreement without the substance that confers legitimacy.[427]

C. The Problem of Ground Truth and Epistemic Circularity

A deeper failure is ground truth.[428] AI learns from labeled examples,[429] but in adjudication what is the ground truth?[430] Past verdicts are products of human judgment, not objective truth, so training on them trains on human bias, error, and historical inequity—the AI learns what juries have decided, not what is true.[431] That is epistemic circularity: using an imperfect institution's outputs as the training signal for its replacement.[432] It launders bias as objectivity—reproducing racial, class, and gender distortions while making them harder to detect because the outputs appear technical, inheriting the jury's weaknesses while shedding its legitimacy.[433] Training on "true" outcomes fails too: exonerations are few and skewed, and most cases have no known ground truth beyond the verdict.[434] The system's epistemic limitation is that it cannot know with certainty what

---

[425] *See* Burrell, *supra* note 322, at 1–5; *see also* Barocas & Selbst, *supra* note 267, at 691–95.
[426] *See* Amar, *supra* note 8, at 1183–87; *see also* de Tocqueville, *supra* note 142, at 270–72.
[427] *See* Searle, *supra* note 56, at 417–24; *see also* Nagel, *supra* note 415, at 435–50.
[428] *See* Surden, *supra* note 5, at 92–99; *see also* Barocas & Selbst, *supra* note 267, at 677–80.
[429] *See* Surden, *supra* note 5, at 92–99; *see also* Goodfellow, et al., *supra* note 333, at 96–105.
[430] *See* Tribe, *supra* note 191, at 1330–36; *see also* Allen & Leiter, *supra* note 12, at 1497–1504.
[431] *See* Kalven & Zeisel, *supra* note 164, at 3–12; *see also* Kahan, *supra* note 376, at 18–25.
[432] *See* Tribe, *supra* note 191, at 1330–36; *see also* Citron, *supra* note 20, at 1267–75.
[433] *See* Citron, *supra* note 20, at 1267–75; *see also* Pasquale, *supra* note 23, at 3–9.
[434] *See* Garrett, *supra* note 348, at 48–52; *see also* Samuel R. Gross et al., Exonerations in the United States 1989 Through 2003, 95 *J. Crim. L. & Criminology* 523, 524–30 (2005).

happened, and AI cannot conjure truth from contested evidence, so its training replicates institutional history rather than discovering reality.[435]

D. Value Alignment and the Limits of Optimization

Even a sophisticated AI jury confronts value alignment.[436] As Brian Christian shows, present-day AI systems often optimize for measurable proxies that diverge from the human goals they serve, because translating complex moral norms into mathematical objectives is a philosophical and societal problem, not merely a technical one.[437] Legal judgment is not a single objective function but competing values—accuracy, fairness, mercy, deterrence, dignity, legitimacy.[438] The criminal system tolerates some wrongful acquittals to avoid wrongful convictions, tort balances compensation against efficiency, and punitive damages blend deterrence with condemnation—none reducible to one metric without controversial normative choices.[439] But AI requires an optimization target: optimize accuracy and the system may become punitive; fairness and it may sacrifice truth-seeking; efficiency and it may undermine due process.[440] The system has a pluralistic moral structure that the jury embodies by injecting human judgment;[441] replacing it requires someone to encode those values, shifting moral authority from citizens to designers.[442] Alignment is thus the central problem: to build an AI jury is to decide what the jury is for—accuracy, legitimacy, participation, accountability.[443] The constitutional tradition answers

---

[435] *See* Tribe, *supra* note 191, at 1330–36; *see also Winship*, 397 U.S. at 363–64.
[436] *See* Stuart Russell, *Human Compatible: Artificial Intelligence and the Problem of Control* 173–79 (Viking 2019); *see also* Brian Christian, *The Alignment Problem: Machine Learning and Human Values* 1–7 (W.W. Norton & Co. 2020).
[437] *See* Christian, *supra* note 434, at 1-7.
[438] *See* Tribe, supra note 191, at 1330–36; *see also* Dworkin, supra note 265, at 1057–63.
[439] *See Winship*, 397 U.S. at 363–64; *see also* 4 Blackstone, supra note ___, at *352.
[440] *See* Surden, supra note 5, at 92–99; *see also* Goodfellow, et al., supra note ___, at 96–105.
[441] *See* Hart, *supra* note 411, at 404–06; *see also* Calabresi, *supra* note 381, at 26–31.
[442] *See* Pasquale, supra note 23, at 3–9; *see also* Citron, *supra* note 20, at 1267–75.
[443] *See* Russell, *supra* note __, at 173–79; *see also* Christian, *supra* note __, at 1–7.

in favor of human responsibility, and substitution would require rewriting that tradition, not merely improving its efficiency.[444] Theoretical architectures fail not because they are computationally impossible but because they cannot escape the epistemic and moral structure of adjudication: they simulate decision-making without replicating the institutional meaning of judgment.[445]

VIII. HYBRID MODELS: AI AS JURY AUGMENTATION

A. AI Evidence Summaries and Timeline Reconstruction

Though unsuited to replace juries, AI may be well suited to assist them.[446] Its most compelling trial application is evidence management, not adjudication.[447] Trials overwhelm jurors because evidence is voluminous, fragmented, and presented in strategic rather than chronological order: dozens of witnesses, piecemeal documents, and exhibits revisited repeatedly, all to be integrated into a timeline while retaining the legal elements—a scale human memory is not designed for.[448] AI can reduce this burden by generating summaries, organizing testimony, reconstructing timelines, highlighting where witnesses agree or diverge, and identifying missing links.[449] Timeline reconstruction is often decisive in complex civil litigation and in criminal cases involving multiple actors or location evidence, helping jurors follow events without becoming

---

[444] *See Duncan*, 391 U.S. at 155–56; *see also* Amar, *supra* note 8, at 1183–87.
[445] *See* Tribe, *supra* note 191, at 1330–36; *see also* Allen & Leiter, *supra* note 12, at 1497–1504.
[446] *See* Citron, *supra* note 20, at 1267–75; *see also* Surden, *supra* note 5, at 92–99.
[447] *See* Maura R. Grossman & Gordon V. Cormack, *Technology-Assisted Review in E-Discovery Can Be More Effective and More Efficient Than Exhaustive Manual Review*, 17 RICH. J.L. & TECH. 11, ¶¶ 2–4 (2011); *see also* Andrew D. Selbst & Solon Barocas, *The Intuitive Appeal of Explainable Machines*, 87 FORDHAM L. REV. 1085, 1090–92 (2018).
[448] *See* Pennington & Hastie, supra note 176, at 242, 242–46; *see also* Hastie, et al., supra note 29, at 22–28.
[449] *See* Grossman & Cormack, *supra* note __, ¶¶ 2–4; *see also* Surden, *supra* note 5, at 92–99.

forensic analysts.[450] The advantage is that these tasks do not require AI to decide truth, only to organize information; if jurors remain responsible for what to believe, the system is a cognitive prosthetic, not a substitute decision-maker.[451] It can reduce reliance on emotionally salient testimony and aid recall, strengthening rather than undermining the jury's epistemic function.[452]

B. Technical Expert Translation and Juror Comprehension

Another role is translating expert evidence. Litigation increasingly depends on technical expertise, and jurors must evaluate dueling experts whose testimony is dense and strategically framed. Courts instruct jurors that they may accept or reject expert testimony,[453] but that is meaningful only if jurors understand it; otherwise they rely on surface cues like confidence and credentials. AI could explain concepts in plain language, define terms, present competing claims side-by-side, and clarify assumptions[454]—helping jurors grasp engineering principles, physiological processes, or regression analysis without interpreting jargon.[455] But this role carries danger: translation can become interpretation.[456] If AI overstates the certainty of disputed claims, jurors may treat its explanation as authoritative, especially since expert disputes often turn on contested assumptions rather than basic concepts.[457] The system needs jurors to understand enough

---

450 *See* John C.P. Goldberg & Benjamin C. Zipursky, *Torts as Wrongs*, 88 TEX. L. REV. 917, 918–24 (2010); *see also* Burns, supra note 342, at 3–7.
451 *See* Surden, supra note 5, at 92–99 (2014); *see also* Bender et al., supra note 44, at 615–17.
452 *See* Pennington & Hastie, *supra* note 176, at 242–46; *see also* Fed. R. Evid. 403.
453 1A O'Malley, *supra* note 92, at § 15:09.
454 See Maura R. Grossman & Gordon V. Cormack, *Technology-Assisted Review in E-Discovery Can Be More Effective and More Efficient Than Exhaustive Manual Review*, 17 RICH. J.L. & TECH. 11, ¶¶ 2–4 (2011); *see also* Surden, supra note 5, at 92–99.
455 *See* Restatement (Third) of Torts: Prods. Liab. § 2 cmt. a (Am. L. Inst. 1998); *see also* David G. Owen, *The Puzzle of Comment j*, 55 HASTINGS L.J. 1377, 1382–86 (2004).
456 *See* Citron, supra note 20, at 1267–75; *see also* Pasquale, supra note 23, at 3–9.
457 *See* Fed. R. Evid. 702 advisory committee's note to 2000 amendment; *see also Daubert,* 509 U.S. at 595.

to evaluate credibility and uncertainty, not to become scientists;[458] AI must therefore communicate uncertainty rather than flatten it, assisting comprehension without presenting contested conclusions as settled fact.[459]

C. The "Thirteenth Juror" Risk and Deference Effects

The greatest risk of augmentation is not that AI will be wrong but that humans will defer to it when it is wrong—automation bias, the tendency to trust machine outputs that appear objective on difficult tasks.[460] In the jury context this is magnified: laypeople in a high-stakes environment may treat an AI summary or suggested conclusion as neutral truth rather than an interpretive artifact.[461] This is the "thirteenth juror" problem: the AI becomes an invisible participant whose authority is not challenged as a human juror's would be, because jurors cannot easily interrogate an algorithm or understand its limits, and its perceived impartiality lets it dominate deliberation.[462] The risk is compounded by the persuasive fluency of AI language, which creates an illusion of correctness and can function as covert advocacy not subject to cross-examination or evidentiary rules.[463] Augmentation therefore demands institutional caution: AI outputs have epistemic gravity, shaping what jurors notice and treat as salient, and a tool that influences salience influences outcomes—so augmentation can quietly become substitution even when the formal decision remains with the jury.[464]

---

458 *See Daubert*, 509 U.S. at 596; *see also* 1A O'Malley, *supra* note 92, at § 15:09.
459 *See* Citron, *supra* note 20, at 1267–75; *see also* Burrell, *supra* note 322, at 1–5.
460 *See* Linda J. Skitka et al., Does Automation Bias Decision-Making?, 51 *Int'l J. Hum.–Comput. Stud.* 991, 992–93 (1999); Citron, *supra* note 20, at 1272–73.
461 *See* Diamond et al., *supra* note 164, at 196–97; Andrew D. Selbst, *Disparate Impact in Big Data Policing*, 52 GA. L. REV. 109, 123–24 (2017).
462 *Cf.* Nancy S. Marder, *The Myth of the Nullifying Jury*, 93 NW. U. L. REV. 877, 885–86 (1999); *See* Hans & Vidmar, *supra* note 6, at 159–63.
463 *See* Michael L. Miller, Persuasion and the Jury, 89 *Judicature* 24, 26–27 (2005); *See* OpenAI, *GPT-4 Technical Report*, *supra* note 304, at 2–3.
464 *See* Coglianese & Lehr, *supra* note 284, at 1186–88; *See* Citron, *supra* note 20, at 1308–09.

D. Designing AI Assistance Without Delegating Judgment

Responsible integration requires one principle: assistance must not become delegation.[465] The jury's legitimacy depends on jurors making the ultimate judgment, so any system that displaces it undermines the jury's role, and design must preserve juror autonomy.[466] First, AI tools must be constrained to the evidentiary record, generating nothing outside admitted exhibits and testimony, with provenance tracking citing support for each statement.[467] Second, outputs should be framed as organizational tools, presenting competing timelines or disputed facts rather than a single narrative.[468] Third, tools must communicate uncertainty explicitly, highlighting ambiguities and contested evidence.[469] Fourth, courts should consider instructions warning against undue reliance, reminding jurors that AI is not a witness, expert, or decision-maker.[470] Fifth, any trial system should be auditable, its outputs logged and reviewable on appeal so courts can assess whether its use undermined fairness.[471] The challenge is to harness AI's strengths without importing its weaknesses into the core of adjudication: the jury decides facts in a publicly acceptable way, and AI assistance can strengthen jurors' capacities only if constrained so that jurors remain the authors of the verdict rather than consumers of algorithmic conclusions.[472]

---

465 *See* Coglianese & Lehr, *supra* note 284, at 1186–88 (2017).
466 *See Duncan*, 391 U.S. at 155–56; Hans & Vidmar, *supra* note 6, at 1–3.
467 *See Turner v. Louisiana*, 379 U.S. 466, 472–73 (1965); *Parker v. Gladden*, 385 U.S. 363, 364–65 (1966).
468 *See* Nancy S. Marder, *Bringing Jury Instructions into the Twenty-First Century*, 81 NOTRE DAME L. REV. 449, 454–56 (2006); *See* Diamond, *supra* note 164, at 568.
469 *See* Parasuraman & Manzey, *supra* note 461, at 386–87; *See* Tversky & Kahneman, *supra* note 36, at 1128.
470 *See* Shari Seidman Diamond et al., Juror Reactions to Jury Instructions: A Field Study, 10 *Psychol. Pub. Pol'y & L.* 189, 196–97 (2004); Fed. R. Evid. 105 (limiting instructions).
471 *See* Pasquale, *supra* note 23, at 140–42; Citron, *supra* note 20, at 1308–09.
472 *See* Coglianese & Lehr, *supra* note 284, at 1186–88; *See* James Oldham, *Trial by Jury: The Seventh Amendment and Anglo-American Special Juries* 1–4 (2006).

IX. THE FUTURE: ACCURACY VS. LEGITIMACY

A. Accuracy vs. Legitimacy

Discussions of AI in adjudication often assume accuracy is the only relevant metric: if a machine predicts guilt more reliably, why not use it?[473] But legal authority derives not from correctness alone but from public acceptance of procedure.[474] Even a demonstrably more accurate machine could undermine legitimacy by turning verdicts into technocratic outputs rather than democratic judgments.[475] "Accuracy" is itself hard to define in adjudication, where ground truth is often unknowable and the jury decides not truth versus falsity but sufficiency of proof.[476] AI that outperforms juries in predicting outcomes may simply be better at replicating historical verdict patterns or detecting persuasive narratives—accuracy as conformity with institutional habit, not correspondence with reality.[477] Legitimacy is a social phenomenon: people accept verdicts reached through a process they recognize as fair, which the jury embodies through participation,

---

[473] *See* Coglianese & Lehr, *supra* note 284, at 1153–55; *See* Richard A. Posner, *An Economic Approach to Legal Procedure and Judicial Administration*, 2 J. LEGAL STUD. 399, 400–02 (1973).
[474] *See* Tom R. Tyler, Procedural Justice, Legitimacy, and the Effective Rule of Law, 30 *Crime & Just.* 283, 284–86 (2003); *See* Lon L. Fuller, *The Morality of Law* 39–41 (rev. ed. 1969).
[475] *See* Citron, *supra* note 20, at 1302–04; James Oldham, *Trial by Jury: The Seventh Amendment and Anglo-American Special Juries* 1–4 (2006).
[476] *See* Harry T. Edwards & Linda A. Elliott, *Beware of Numbers* , 80 CORNELL L. REV. 1197, 1203–05 (1995); *See* Ronald J. Allen & Michael S. Pardo, *The Problematic Value of Mathematical Models of Evidence*, 36 J. LEGAL STUD. 107, 109–10 (2007).
[477] *See* Jon Kleinberg et al., Human Decisions and Machine Predictions, 133 *Q.J. Econ.* 237, 240–42 (2018); *See* Andrew D. Selbst et al., Fairness and Abstraction in Sociotechnical Systems, 2 *Proc. Conf. Fairness, Accountability & Transparency* 59, 60–61 (2019).

deliberation, and transparency.[478] Efficiency is not adjudication's primary moral value; the criminal system is optimized not for conviction but for legitimacy in the face of coercive power.[479]

B. The Jury as Democratic Technology

The jury is better described as a democratic technology: a mechanism by which the state converts public participation into legitimate coercion.[480] It lets ordinary citizens apply the law, transforming adjudication from an elite bureaucratic act into a communal one—a structural function distinguishing American adjudication from administrative governance.[481] It also educates citizens in evidence, doubt, and the seriousness of judgment; as Tocqueville saw, service habituates citizens to self-government, making the jury part of the civic architecture of the republic.[482] Replacing juries with AI would change civic participation itself, removing one of the few mechanisms by which citizens directly participate in state power.[483] Substitution is therefore politically and morally destabilizing even where epistemically plausible: it shifts adjudication from democracy to administration, signals that truth is determined by systems rather than citizens, and reduces the trial from a ritual of accountability to algorithmic classification, weakening the cultural legitimacy of law.[484]

C. Embodied AI and the Possibility of Future Substitution

---

[478] *See* Tyler, *supra* note 474, at 284–86; *See* id. at 286–90.
[479] *See* Guido Calabresi & A. Douglas Melamed, *Property Rules, Liability Rules, and Inalienability*, 85 HARV. L. REV. 1089, 1094–95 (1972); *See Winship*, 397 U.S. at 372 (Harlan, J., concurring).
[480] *See* Amar, *supra* note 8, at 1183–90; Oldham, *supra* note 473, at 1–4.
[481] *See Duncan*, 391 U.S. at 155–56; Hans & Vidmar, *supra* note 6, at 1–3.
[482] *See* de Tocqueville, *supra* note 142, at 273–76; *See* Hans & Vidmar, *supra* note 6, at 161–63.
[483] *See* Citron, *supra* note 20, at 1302–04; See id.
[484] *See* Tom R. Tyler, Procedural Justice, Legitimacy, and the Effective Rule of Law, 30 *Crime & Just.* 283, 284–86 (2003); *See Atlas Roofing*, 430 U.S. at 450.

One might object that these limitations are contingent, not permanent.[485] AI is improving rapidly, with better calibration, grounding, and multimodal reasoning, and future systems integrating sensory input, persistent memory, and real-world verification might reduce hallucination and increase reliability.[486] If AI became more embodied—acquiring situated interaction with the world—it might approximate human judgment more closely.[487] This objection has force: a future system might process evidence rigorously, detect deception reliably, model causation accurately, and articulate reasons satisfying transparency concerns, in which case the epistemic case against substitution would weaken.[488] But even if epistemic substitution becomes possible, normative substitution may remain undesirable: the jury is a tool for legitimacy, not merely truth, and its function is not exhausted by reaching correct outcomes but embodies democratic responsibility and the community's authorization of coercion—value that persists even if machines become better reasoners.[489]

D. Why Replacement May Be Undesirable Even If It Becomes Possible

Even with more accurate verdicts, replacing juries would alter the moral character of adjudication.[490] Trials are rituals of accountability requiring human beings to confront evidence, doubt, and the consequences of condemnation—a morally significant process that forces society

---

[485] *See* Henry E. Smith, *Modularity in Contracts: Boilerplate and Information Flow*, 104 MICH. L. REV. 1175, 1178–79 (2006).
[486] *See* OpenAI, *GPT-4 Technical Report*, arXiv:2303.08774, at 1–3 (2023); Tom B. Brown et al., Language Models Are Few-Shot Learners, 33 *Advances in Neural Info. Processing Sys.* 1877, 1878–80 (2020).
[487] *See* Rodney A. Brooks, Intelligence Without Representation, 47 *Artificial Intelligence* 139, 141–43 (1991).
[488] *Cf.* David J. Hand, *The Improbability Principle* 3–5 (2014); *See* Stuart Russell & Peter Norvig, *Artificial Intelligence: A Modern Approach* 1–4 (4th ed. 2021).
[489] *See* Tyler, *supra* note 474, at 284–86; *See Duncan*, 391 U.S. at 155–56.
[490] *See* Tyler, *supra* note 474, at 284–86; Citron, *supra* note 20, at 1302–04.

to bear responsibility for punishment and makes coercion communal rather than bureaucratic.[491] AI substitution would turn punishment into administration, letting society distance itself from the moral weight of conviction: if an algorithm convicts, no citizen must say "I am willing to imprison this person," and the decision becomes a technical output rather than a moral act—allowing the state to wield coercion without the human burden of judgment.[492] It would also introduce legitimacy crises, with defendants challenging the system as biased and unaccountable and public trust eroding if outputs are seen as controlled by corporations or technocrats.[493] The jury, despite its flaws, is culturally intelligible: people understand jurors as imperfect humans trying their best, which creates tolerance for error that AI does not enjoy—a machine is expected to be right, and when wrong is not merely mistaken but illegitimate.[494] Even if substitution becomes feasible, the deeper question remains whether we want a system in which judgment is outsourced. The jury trial is one of the last institutional spaces where citizens collectively authorize coercion, and removing it would change the relationship between citizen and state.[495]

X. INSTITUTIONAL DESIGN AND MODES OF ADJUDICATIVE REASONING

Debates over AI substitution often treat adjudication as a purely technical activity: weighing evidence, calculating probabilities, and selecting the most likely account. So framed, replacement of human fact-finders by superior pattern-recognizers appears inevitable. But this misunderstands adjudication as an institutional design problem rather than a computational one. Courts are not information-processing systems but institutional arrangements designed to produce

---

491 *See* Burns, *supra* note 342, at 1–4; *See* Hans & Vidmar, *supra* note 6, at 159–63.
492 *See Atlas Roofing Co. v. Occupational Safety & Health Review Comm'n*, 430 U.S. 442, 450 (1977); Citron, *supra* note 20, at 1302–04.
493 *See* Pasquale, *supra* note 23, at 140–42; *See* id.
494 *See* Hans & Vidmar, *supra* note 6, at 1–3; *See* id. at 161–63.
495 *See* Amar, *supra* note 8, at 1183–90; *See* Oldham, *supra* note 473, at 1–4.

authoritative judgments under uncertainty,[496] so the question requires comparing the decision-making logic of the institutions that perform adjudication. Three modes can be distinguished: jury reasoning, judicial reasoning, and algorithmic reasoning, each with a different epistemic logic.

A. Jury Reasoning: Narrative Judgment and Democratic Legitimacy

Juries reason in a way both narrative and social. Research consistently shows jurors construct narrative explanations rather than evaluating isolated propositions or probabilities, integrating evidence into a coherent account and selecting the most plausible story consistent with ordinary human behavior.[497] This is intertwined with moral evaluation, since negligence, recklessness, intent, and reasonableness are normative judgments requiring community standards.[498] The jury is thus a moral interpreter, and its verdict a collective judgment that a version of events is proven to a legally sufficient degree. Group deliberation distributes responsibility and subjects individual judgments to social scrutiny, so the verdict's legitimacy derives not solely from accuracy but from the democratic character of the process.

B. Judicial Reasoning: Doctrinal Analysis and Legal Formalism

Judges reason through doctrine rather than narrative plausibility alone, interpreting statutes, applying precedent, and articulating rules consistent with the legal system. Even as fact-finders in bench trials, they express reasoning through doctrinal categories subject to appellate review, so judicial legitimacy derives largely from adherence to legal principle rather than democratic participation. Judges rely on narrative and are not immune to bias, but institutional

---

[496] Mirjan R. Damaška, *Evidence Law Adrift* 3–10 (1997).
[497] Nancy Pennington & Reid Hastie, *A Cognitive Theory of Juror Decision Making: The Story Model*, 13 CARDOZO L. REV. 519, 521–29 (1991).
[498] See Ronald J. Allen & Michael S. Pardo, *The Problematic Value of Mathematical Models of Evidence*, 36 J. Legal Stud. 107, 111–14 (2007); Ronald J. Allen & Michael S. Pardo, *Relative Plausibility and Its Critics*, 23 Int'l J. Evidence & Proof 5, 7–9 (2019).

expectations require translating reasoning into the language of doctrine, imposing a structure that differs from jury deliberation.

C. Algorithmic Reasoning: Statistical Optimization

AI systems reason differently again, identifying statistical patterns in data and generating predictions by optimizing functions that minimize error, without reasoning through narrative coherence or doctrine.[499] A model trained on historical outcomes maps inputs to probability estimates without evaluating the moral significance of conduct. This offers advantages—processing vast information, detecting subtle patterns, producing consistent outputs—but its epistemic logic differs fundamentally from adjudication: it optimizes predictive accuracy from past data, whereas fact-finding reconstructs unique historical events, and statistical optimization does not incorporate the normative judgments central to legal determinations.

D. Institutional Implications

Recognizing these modes clarifies why an "AI jury" is conceptually problematic. Replacing juries would not substitute one decision-maker for another but replace one institutional logic with a fundamentally different one: narrative reasoning grounded in experience giving way to statistical inference, and moral evaluation through community judgment giving way to optimization defined by programmers and datasets. This raises questions of legitimacy as well as accuracy, since jury authority rests partly on community participation; algorithmic judgments would shift authority toward technical expertise and might lack social legitimacy even at high accuracy. The relevant inquiry is thus not the comparative cognitive performance of humans and machines but whether algorithmic reasoning can replicate the epistemic and normative functions

---

[499] See Stuart Russell & Peter Norvig, *Artificial Intelligence: A Modern Approach* 19–28, 695–706 (4th ed. 2021); Harry Surden, Machine Learning and Law, 89 WASH. L. REV. 87, 90–97 (2014).

juries perform—and at present there is little evidence it can. AI may assist by organizing information and translating technical material, but the institutional logic of adjudication remains fundamentally human.

XI. THE STRONGEST CASE FOR ALGORITHMIC ADJUDICATION

The argument for replacing juries is not merely speculative. A growing body of research suggests algorithmic systems may outperform humans in prediction under uncertainty. Advocates rely on three claims: that predictive models outperform human judgment, that algorithms produce greater consistency, and that machine reasoning reduces bias.[500]

A. Predictive Accuracy and the Superiority of Statistical Models

Research since early work in decision science repeatedly finds that simple statistical models equal or exceed expert judgment in domains like medical diagnosis and behavioral prediction, and machine learning extends this by detecting complex relationships humans cannot.[501] Scholarship applying these insights predicts judicial outcomes with notable accuracy, including Supreme Court cases from issue area and voting patterns, and bail, sentencing, and recidivism forecasts.[502] If adjudication were primarily predictive—determining which account is

---

500 See Paul E. Meehl, *Clinical Versus Statistical Prediction* 21–40 (1954); Daniel Kahneman, *Thinking, Fast and Slow* 222–27 (2011).
501 See Daniel Martin Katz, Michael J. Bommarito II & Josh Blackman, *A General Approach for Predicting the Behavior of the Supreme Court of the United States*, 12 PLOS ONE e0174698 (2017); Nikolaos Aletras et al., *Predicting Judicial Decisions of the European Court of Human Rights*, 2 Peer J Computer Sci. e93 (2016).
502 Daniel Martin Katz, Michael J. Bommarito II & Josh Blackman, *A General Approach for Predicting the Behavior of the Supreme Court of the United States*, 12 PLOS ONE e0174698 (2017); Jon Kleinberg et al., *Human Decisions and Machine Predictions*, 133 Q.J. Econ. 237 (2018).

most likely correct—these developments would support replacing human decision-makers, and the jury's reliance on intuition might appear inefficient beside statistical rigor.

B. Consistency and the Reduction of Arbitrary Decision-Making

Legal outcomes vary with factors unrelated to merits—the identity of the judge, jury composition, even fatigue and time of day, as studies of parole decisions suggest. Algorithms apply the same rule to every case regardless of such factors, offering consistency proponents tie to the rule of law: standardized decision rules could produce more uniform, predictable outcomes than the variability of deliberation.

C. The Promise of Bias Reduction

Human decision-makers are subject to documented biases—confirmation bias, anchoring, implicit stereotypes—that affect how jurors weigh evidence and credibility. Proponents argue algorithms relying on formal decision rules could be less susceptible to implicit bias and, trained on curated data, could evaluate evidence without regard to race, gender, or status. This argument has been influential in criminal justice, where risk-assessment tools are presented as reducing disparities, suggesting substitution might appear not only feasible but desirable.

D. The Limits of the Algorithmic Case

Together these arguments are powerful: machine learning detects patterns humans miss, applies rules consistently, and may reduce some biases, and in domains defined by prediction these advantages have driven wide adoption. Yet they rest on a crucial assumption—that the jury's task is fundamentally predictive. The next Part challenges that assumption. Legal fact-finding reconstructs unique historical events and evaluates conduct against normative standards; once understood this way, the advantages of algorithmic reasoning become less decisive.

XII. WHY PREDICTIVE ACCURACY DOES NOT JUSTIFY ALGORITHMIC ADJUDICATION

The arguments for algorithmic adjudication depend on treating adjudication as prediction. Examined closely, that assumption fails: the advantages of algorithmic reasoning arise in predicting across large datasets, whereas trials reconstruct unique events and evaluate conduct normatively.

A. Prediction Versus Reconstruction

Machine learning excels at prediction by identifying statistical relationships across many examples. But trials ask what occurred in the past, not what will happen. Fact-finders reconstruct events that are unique, context-dependent, and poorly documented, assembling fragments into a coherent account of a particular episode.[503] Statistical prediction is poorly suited to this: models rely on patterns across many cases, but legal disputes turn on singular facts that may never appear in training data. Prior cases are not repeated observations of the same event; each presents a distinctive combination of circumstances, so the predictive paradigm does not map onto the jury's epistemic task.[504]

B. The Limits of Consistency

Consistency alone is not a virtue: a system that consistently produces unjust outcomes is not improved by uniformity. And apparent consistency may mislead, since models derive predictions from training data reflecting historical decisions; where past decisions contain bias, the

---

[503] See Mirjan R. Damaška, *Evidence Law Adrift* 3–10 (1997); Larry Laudan, *Truth, Error, and Criminal Law* 13–20 (2006).
[504] Tribe, *supra* note 191, at 1329. Ronald J. Allen & Michael S. Pardo, Relative Plausibility and Its Critics, 23 Int'l J. Evidence & Proof 5 (2019).

model encodes it, reproducing disparities with greater efficiency.[505] Human decision-making contains self-correction that algorithms may lack—jurors deliberate, challenge interpretations, and revise conclusions, so some variability reflects openness to reconsideration rather than defect.[506]

C. Bias and the Illusion of Algorithmic Neutrality

The claim that algorithms eliminate bias is more complicated than it appears. Machine learning depends on training data that often reflect inequality and discrimination, which models may reproduce or amplify.[507] Systems also require designers to choose variables, representations, and objective functions—choices embedding normative judgments about desirable outcomes and error distribution, so algorithmic decision-making relocates human judgment to system design rather than eliminating it.[508] Opacity compounds the problem: complex models produce accurate predictions with limited transparency, undermining procedural fairness where parties need to understand and challenge a decision.[509]

D. Adjudication as Normative Judgment

The most fundamental difficulty is the normative character of legal determinations. Negligence, recklessness, intent, and reasonableness require evaluative judgments about conduct, not merely descriptive findings; jurors consider not only what happened but whether it violates standards embedded in law. These judgments are contextual—assessing reasonableness requires

---

505 Solon Barocas & Andrew D. Selbst, *Big Data's Disparate Impact*, 104 CALIF. L. REV. 671 (2016); Cathy O'Neil, *Weapons of Math Destruction* 3–16 (2016).
506 Citron, *supra* note 20, at 1249; Pasquale, *supra* note 23.
507 Solon Barocas & Andrew D. Selbst, *Big Data's Disparate Impact*,104 CALIF. L. REV. 671 (2016). Pauline T. Kim, *Data-Driven Discrimination at Work*, 58 WM. & MARY L. REV. 857 (2017). Mayson, *supra* note 268, at 2218.
508 Jon Kleinberg et al., *Discrimination in the Age of Algorithms*,10 J. Legal Analysis 113 (2018). Finale Doshi-Velez & Been Kim, *Towards a Rigorous Science of Interpretable Machine Learning,* arXiv (2017).
509 See Mirjan R. Damaška, *Evidence Law Adrift* 3–10 (1997); Larry Laudan, *Truth, Error, and Criminal Law* 13–20 (2006).

weighing the circumstances, community expectations, and the values in the standard—and cannot be reduced to correlations from past cases. The jury's role reflects the democratic character of the institution: placing citizens at the center ensures community standards shape the meaning of legal norms, whereas replacing juries would shift interpretive authority to the designers of models.

E. The Enduring Role of the Jury

The advantages of machine learning do not translate directly into adjudication. Trials require reconstructing unique events, evaluating credibility, and applying normative standards reflecting community values—social, contextual, interpretive tasks. AI may nonetheless support fact-finders by organizing evidence, identifying inconsistencies, and translating technical material, enhancing the jury's capacity without displacing its judgment. The question is not whether AI can contribute to adjudication—it can—but whether it can replace the jury without transforming the nature of legal judgment. Such a transformation would fundamentally alter the epistemic and institutional foundations of the trial.

CONCLUSION

Artificial intelligence has made jury substitution newly plausible, and juries have real weaknesses—bias, fatigue, susceptibility to emotional persuasion, and difficulty with technical evidence. From a purely computational perspective, the case for AI assistance is strong. But the jury is not merely a computational device. It is an epistemic institution performing a hybrid function: assessing credibility, synthesizing narratives, and applying burdens of proof that are moral, not merely probabilistic. It decides not what is likely but what is sufficiently proven to justify coercion; it does not merely reconstruct events but assigns responsibility; it does not merely output conclusions but produces legitimacy through democratic participation. These functions are inseparable, and the jury's epistemic authority is tied to its normative role as the community's voice in judgment.

Modern generative AI remains epistemically unfit to replace this institution. Its tendency toward hallucination is a structural mismatch with adjudication, which requires disciplined refusal to fill gaps rather than fluent completion. AI also struggles with relevance, explainability, and adversarial manipulation—problems magnified in litigation, where strategic behavior is guaranteed—and lacks both the embodied social understanding credibility requires and the moral responsibility legal judgment presupposes. "Human-in-the-loop" safeguards are inadequate here, because the jury's function is not to supervise outputs but to exercise independent, collective judgment about credibility, narrative coherence, and blameworthiness.[510] A reviewer who rubber-stamps algorithmic conclusions cannot replicate the deliberative process that gives verdicts their legitimacy; if the machine structures the narrative and frames the inferences, the human presence becomes cosmetic rather than constitutive.

This does not mean AI has no courtroom role. It may become indispensable as a tool for juries—organizing evidence, reconstructing timelines, clarifying expert testimony, and reducing overload—and, properly constrained, could strengthen the jury's epistemic function. But that role must be designed to avoid creating a "thirteenth juror" whose outputs dominate deliberation through automation bias and rhetorical authority. Ultimately the question is not whether AI can compute truth more efficiently but whether legal truth is the kind of thing that can be computed at all. In the American system, truth is not merely discovered but constructed through human

---

510 Finale Doshi-Velez & Been Kim, *Towards A Rigorous Science of Interpretable ML*, arXiv (2017); Selbst & Barocas, *The Intuitive Appeal of Explainable Machines*, 87 FORDHAM L. REV. 1085 (2018).

judgment under procedural constraint, and the jury trial is a mechanism not only for decision but for accountability. Until AI can distinguish truth from plausibility, resist manipulation, and bear the moral weight of condemnation, it cannot substitute for the jury without undermining both the epistemic foundations and democratic legitimacy of adjudication. Even if progress eventually enables machines to replicate aspects of human reasoning, replacing juries would transform the meaning of adjudication: the jury is not merely an inefficient information processor but a civic institution through which society assumes responsibility for the exercise of legal power. Its persistence may reflect not technological backwardness but institutional wisdom. AI may reshape the trial, but the verdict must remain human.

ABOUT THE AUTHOR

Daniel S. Alcorn is a management-side labor and employment law attorney licensed in Texas, Arizona and Illinois. He currently practices Of Counsel with Davis & Campbell L.L.C. in Peoria, Illinois, where he maintains a subfocus in Artificial Intelligence law and policy. Dan previously practiced with Littler Mendelson P.C., the world's largest management-side labor and employment law firm, after serving as Associate General Counsel – Employment Law for TORC Robotics, Inc.

in Austin, Texas and in-house employment law counsel for State Farm Mutual Automobile Insurance Company in Bloomington, Illinois.

Dan has authored numerous legal articles published in law reviews, bar journals and other legal publications. Additionally, Dan has published several fiction and nonfiction works and novels.

Dan earned his B.A. in economics and philosophy from Knox College and his J.D. from Drake University Law School, where he served as Articles Editor of the Drake Law Review. More recently, Dan earned his graduate certificate from M.I.T. in Artificial Intelligence and its implications for business strategy. He is the founder and publisher of Sterling Letter Press, which champions writers who create works, fiction and nonfiction, which sit at the intersection of law, ethics, and the messier truths of human character, with the discipline of an argument and the pulse of a story.

Dan is married to Marcy Alcorn, and between them they have five wonderful children and one granddaughter with another grandchild on the way.